PUBLISH YOUR FIRST
DIGITAL MAGAZINE

Taking You from
Concept to Delivery

by
Lorraine Phillips

360 Books
Atlanta, GA

For direct links to ALL the resources
listed throughout this book,
please visit:

WWW.
first
digital
magazine
.com

Author: Lorraine Phillips
Editor: Samantha Grace Dias

ISBN-10: 0-9889535-0-1
ISBN-13: 978-0-9889535-0-5

LCCN: 2013902788
Library of Congress subject headings:
1. Magazine publishing.
2. Digital publishing.
3. Digital media---United States.

Published by:
360 Books, LLC
PO Box 105603, #22430
Atlanta, GA 30348-5603
www.3sixtybooks.com

First Printing
Printed in the United States of America

Dedicated to all the visionaries:
the ones who see past what is and
stubbornly live in the realms of what could be.

Use this books organizational
structure to design research
structure and development structure.

Table of Contents

Chapter 2: Planning Your Magazine

Chapter 3: Finding Content and Images

Chapter 4: Your Online Presence

Chapter 5: Preparing Search Engine-Friendly Web Pages

Chapter 6: Using Social Media

Chapter 7: Creating Your Magazine's Website

Chapter 8: Creating Your Magazine's Blog

Chapter 9: Digital Magazine Design

Chapter 10: Creating and Proofing Your Digital Magazine

Chapter 11: Monetizing Your Magazine

Chapter 12: Keeping It Legal

Appendix A: Essential WordPress Plug-ins 159

Appendix B: Industry News and Resources 167

Introduction

The explosive growth of smartphones and tablets means that the way we consume media has forever been changed. With readers quickly migrating to digital, newspaper and magazine newsstand sales are on the decline. According to Gfk Mediamark Research & Intelligence's "Survey of the American Consumer," readership of digital-only magazines is on the rise; with an increase of 47 percent between the fall of 2011 and 2012, going from 4.4 million people to more than 13.5 million during that time. With this acceleration likely to continue, PwC Global Entertainment and Media Outlook has predicted that consumer spending on digital magazines will reach $611 million by 2015.

The future indeed looks rosy, and as our habits begin to change, it is only inevitable that the money will follow. Recent surveys reveal that 60 percent of advertisers are less interested in print than they were a year ago. But don't count print out just yet; it is far from dead, and you will find many arguing about the predicted longevity of this much loved medium. Some of you who are already producing a print magazine will likely be considering launching a digital version as a complement to your print offering and a way of providing your readers with the best of both worlds. Other print publishers may be considering completely transitioning over to digital as a cheaper alternative to publishing in print. And lastly, there will be those who are interested in creating a digital-only publication, with the possibility of moving to print after an audience has been established.

Either way, a myriad of options are available for creating a digital publication. Will you have a website or blog, create a flip book or app, and how will you distribute your magazine? Various solutions will be presented throughout this book, but I do not for one minute claim this to be the be-all and end-all. My intention is to give you a good place to start by focusing on the most popular tools that exist today and providing you with enough information that you can further explore and evaluate in order to select a solution that works best for you. The options presented are aimed at publishers who don't necessarily have tens of thousands of dollars to spend in creating a publication from scratch but are looking for cost-effective, reasonably easy-to-use solutions.

Other important considerations for a digital publisher will be creating content that is search engine friendly, effectively incorporating social media as a part of a magazine's overall marketing strategy, and finding ways to monetize a magazine; all of which will be covered throughout the course of this book. Know that this has not been written to be read in any particular order, and I suspect that most of you will jump around and read the subjects that are most conducive to where you are in the process. However, I do recommend that you read this in its entirety, as the ideas presented are not mutually exclusive to each chapter. You may read an idea in the website chapter that you will consider implementing on your blog or vice versa. And even though this book covers a wide range of disciplines, they will all come together in helping you produce . . . well . . . the magazine of your dreams.

In closing, I'd just like to add that we've all heard the quote "life is a journey and not a destination"; but most of the time we're so caught up in focusing on the destination (which rarely ever turns out exactly as we expect it to anyway) that we forget to enjoy the journey, which is more often than not the longest part. The journey is what's happening right now, here, today—and more than likely tomorrow too. So don't wait . . . start enjoying it now. Begin to think of your journey *as* the destination. The fact that you're reading this means that you're ready, so have fun. Learn, grow, create, and share. Welcome to the digital magazine revolution.

Lorraine Phillips, Author

Chapter 1:

Magazine Business Fundamentals

What Is a Magazine?

"A magazine is not just a pound of paper. A magazine is a bunch of people with special interests and ideas communicating with a larger group who share the dedication to those interests."

–John Mack Carter

I am not sure how close to the truth John Mack Carter realized he was when he made this statement back in 1981. Thirty-something years later, he was absolutely right: a magazine is not just a pound of paper. Magazines exist in numerous formats today—from print to web, from blog to flip book and even app; and as our technology continues to evolve, who knows the formats we may see in the future. It's an exciting time for all, where the barriers to entry are literally nonexistent and almost everyone on the planet has the ability to be either a publisher or a content creator at will.

what we have in common> Gary

A digital magazine is a highly interactive digital interpretation of a print magazine that can be read on an electronic device such as a computer, laptop, tablet, e-reader, or smartphone. In addition to presenting text and images, a digital magazine enhances the user experience by adding video, audio, animation, and hyperlinks that give instantaneous access to related content and bonus materials.

With the major differences being the medium through which it is delivered and the ability to engage readers through the use of dynamic, interactive elements, a digital magazine mirrors a print magazine in that it is focused around a particular subject; is aimed at a market segment that shares a common interest; is comprised of departments, columns, and features; publishes according to a set schedule or editorial calendar; features high-quality, curated content that is created and crafted by a professional editorial team; and–for the most part–contains original material.

The benefits of launching a digital magazine as opposed to a print publication can include the following:

- Allows for fun, engaging, interactive, immersive content
- Low barriers to entry
- Zero print costs (which is oftentimes the most costly expense associated with producing a print publication)
- Worldwide distribution capabilities and efficiencies that far exceed the ability of print
- Analytics and tracking data that provides much more insight and information than print has ever been able to offer
- Low costs and overhead that allow a digital magazine to sustain itself on a much lower amount of revenue and still remain profitable
- Immediate access to content upon subscription
- Guaranteed delivery to subscribers (meaning no more lost or damaged issues in the mail)
- Back catalogs can be archived with minimal effort and made available for immediate access
- The ability for articles to be indexed by major search engines, which make them more easily discoverable online

- Search and bookmarking capability on magazine content
- Can provide links to additional content or bonus materials
- Ability to link directly to advertiser websites and products
- Conducive to "word-of-mouse" and viral marketing techniques, as readers are able to easily and conveniently share content with the click of a button
- Readers can click through and join conversations that are taking place in forums or on social networks to discuss specific articles or relevant topics of interest
- The capacity to have two-way, on-going, real-time conversations with readers and prospective subscribers
- The ability to be more responsive to reader wants and demands
- Due to the nature of the medium, content can be published more frequently and in a much more timely fashion
- Allows for an environment-friendly, green business model

With the digital magazine industry in its early infancy stage, there are a significant number of challenges that a publisher will have to face and find ways to overcome. One such obstacle includes the lack of solid, proven business models that can be used as case studies and learning tools. Additionally, low barriers to entry means that a digital magazine will have to offer premium, compelling content and innovative design features that can help to differentiate itself from others in the marketplace. Other concerns might be the inability to grow readership without possessing significant Internet marketing skills; the fact that audience measurement standards have not yet been defined for digital-only publications, making it extremely difficult to communicate audience value to advertisers; and getting advertiser buy-in from an industry that is more familiar with print standards. Lastly, there will always be those who just love a glossy. Although you will be creating some type of digital offering, I think it's important to understand the basics of the print magazine business as will be discussed in this chapter.

The Three Types of Magazines

There are three types of print magazines:

Consumer magazines: Consumer magazines are general or special interest magazines that are marketed to the public. The main purpose of these types of magazines is to entertain, sell products, and promote viewpoints. More often than not, they contain some form of advertising. Examples of consumer magazines include *Reader's Digest*, *i-D*, and *O, The Oprah Magazine*.

Trade magazines: Trade magazines are business-to-business magazines whose audience consists of readers in a particular trade or profession. Most will contain technical jargon not easily consumed by the general public. Although some trade magazines may be available on newsstands (e.g., *ComputerUser*, *Communication Arts*, etc.), most are sold through subscription only. Examples of trade magazines include *AJN: American Journal of Nursing* and *Cognitive Psychology*.

Other: Magazines that cannot be defined as being either consumer or trade fall into this category.

Organizational Structure

Although you may be a one-man (or one-woman) team, a print magazine will typically comprise the following departments. I have listed them in what I consider to be the order of importance. My reasoning is that the business department is responsible for planning, strategizing, and putting all the necessary parts together that should allow for a magazine to be profitable; and all other departments will follow and get direction from there.

Editorial, design, and production are responsible for creating a publication that will resonate with the target audience, who will in turn be made aware of the magazine's existence through effective marketing and promotions. Circulation is responsible for pulling in the numbers to attract advertisers. And lastly, the administration department provides support by performing general housekeeping duties.

Who Can Filled these roles?

Business: Responsible for the overall strategic vision and direction of the publication.

Editorial: Accountable for the magazine's content and tone.

Design: Visually creates the look and style of the magazine.

Production: Physically or technically produces the magazine on budget and to specification.

Promotion: Publicizes and advertises the magazine to advertisers; advertising agencies; potential readers; trade, professional, and business entities; interest groups; and other constituencies that are served by the magazine.

Circulation: Acquires, finds, and keeps readers through single-copy sales, subscriptions, free distribution, or other means.

Advertising: Handles, sells, and manages the magazine's advertising, which is often vital to its survival and success. This may be the only revenue source for most trade and business magazines.

Administration: Keeps the books, pays the bills, invoices advertisers, processes payroll, completes forms, and generates reports.

Positions and Duties

CREATIVE *which an be Combined.*

Editor in Chief/Editorial Director: Responsible for setting the vision, tone, style, look, and feel of the publication. Plans and directs the editorial process from concept through to publication. The official go-to person for any editorial issues. Duties may include writing articles, developing story ideas, approving layouts, as well as assisting with business strategic planning and development.

Executive Editor: Reports directly to the editorial director. Performs both managerial and editorial duties, keeping the magazine on schedule by enforcing strict deadlines. He or she also pitches in by preparing, assigning, and editing articles and doing whatever else is necessary to keep the magazine on track and on time.

Senior Editor: Writes, edits, proofreads, and copyedits articles. Helps assign articles to writers, making sure they understand the specific requirements. Other names for this title can include feature editor, beauty editor, fashion editor, and so forth.

Associate Editor: A staff editorial person who supports and assists the editor by writing, editing, and assigning material as required. May also be responsible for composing titles, subtitles, and captions.

Staff Writer: Resident staff member who writes and contributes articles to the magazine.

Contributing Editor: These writers are experts in the field that the magazine covers. This title may also be given to regular freelance writers with whom the magazine wishes to maintain a relationship.

Fact-Checker: Researches submitted articles, checking them for accuracy and correctness.

Copy Editor: Copy editors are not proofreaders. They check written material in its original form before layout and design, looking for and correcting errors in grammar, spelling, usage, and style. They also check articles for form, length, and completeness.

Proofreader: Checks over the final proof for typographical and mechanical errors.

Editorial Assistant: An entry-level position that supports more senior editors. Duties include researching information, setting up interviews, returning calls, making copies, and filing.

Website Editor: Responsible for creating and editing web content.

Creative Director/Art Director: Oversees the artistic design of the magazine and works closely with the editorial director to ensure the design is consistent with the editorial philosophy.

Graphic Designer: A graphic designer (also known as a graphic artist or communications designer) plans, analyzes, and creates visual solutions to communications problems. On a magazine, the graphic designer is responsible for physically creating exactly what the art director envisions, using color, type, illustration, photography, and various print and layout techniques to create a design that effectively communicates and appeals to its intended audience.

Photo Editor: Responsible for assigning visuals and images to magazine stories. Can also be tasked with maintaining, cataloging, and storing images.

BUSINESS

Publisher: Oversees the business side of the magazine and is ultimately responsible for the magazine's profitability. Duties include budgeting, strategic planning, and ad development.

Circulation Director: Manages all paid circulation and is responsible for maintaining and expanding readership.

Marketing Director/Promotions Director: Responsible for publicity and promotions. For a magazine to be successful, it must sell itself to both readers and advertisers.

Production Director: Responsible for creating, coordinating, and overseeing the production schedule to ensure the magazine is produced on time. Helps staff members format material so that all pages are complete and technically accurate. May also oversee the press run.

Advertising Director: Manages a staff of ad sales reps and is responsible for generating advertising in the magazine through direct selling and promotional activities.

Ad Sales Rep: Makes actual sales calls to and sets up appointments with existing and prospective advertisers. Responsible for maintaining current accounts and generating new business.

Business Manager: Supervises internal office management and affairs.

ADDITIONAL ROLES FOR DIGITAL

Programmer/Web Developer/Webmaster: Responsible or the creation and technical upkeep of a site. May specialize in programming languages such as HTML, CSS, JavaScript, PHP, AJAX, and others.

WordPress Developer: Specializes in installing or creating WordPress themes, widgets, and plug-ins. May edit and customize existing themes or create one from scratch to specification. Typical skills for the position include HTML, CSS, PHP, SQL, and JavaScript. (Depending on the content management system selected, this title could also be Drupal Developer, Joomla Developer, and so forth.)

Graphical User Interface Designer/UX Designer: Responsible for designing visuals (such as windows, icons, and menus) for an interface that provides users with the best possible experience and allows for simple, efficient, intuitive actions.

Animator: Adds interactive elements (such as quizzes and polls) to a publication through animations that are usually created using Flash, JavaScript, or HTML5.

Videographer: Records, edits, and produces video projects using equipment and software.

Audio Engineer: Records, edits, and mixes audio sound using equipment and software.

Social Media Strategist: Experienced with social media platforms such as Facebook, Twitter, Pinterest, YouTube, and Google+. Responsible for implementing strategies that increase brand awareness, generate incoming traffic, encourage reader loyalty, and boost subscription sales.

Data Analyst: Responsible for collecting and analyzing data on website performance as well as magazine usage and viewing statistics. Prepares reports and makes recommendations as appropriate.

Departments, Columns, and Features

A magazine's editorial content is divided into three types:

Departments: These are the parts or sections of the magazine that the reader becomes familiar with and expects to see in every issue. They offer consistency and establish the tone and voice of a publication. A department may be written by a different contributor every month. They should be well planned and executed and grouped together under one common topic so that an individual department may have from one to several articles.

Columns: These articles are usually written by an expert or by a famous or respected individual. They provide credibility for the magazine and are written by the same person every issue.

Features: These are the longer pieces in the magazine, usually four to six pages in length. They are unique to every issue and most clearly exhibit the magazine's philosophy.

Reasons for Failure and Success

Failure rates for print magazines are extremely hard to come by. A study performed approximately ten years ago by industry expert, Samir A. Husni estimated that 60 percent of new magazines fail within their first year. Mr. Husni found that if a magazine managed to make it past the first year, they would actually increase their chances for survival down the line. Further statistics revealed that 80 percent of magazines failed by their fourth year, with 90 percent failing by their tenth.

More recent studies conducted by The College of Saint Rose librarian Steve Black (author of *Library Journal*'s 2007 and 2008 "Best New Magazines of the Year" column) indicated that 34 percent of newly launched magazines that fell into the "best new magazine" category failed within the first five years, with 13 percent of those failing within the first. These numbers continue to rise, and as with most industries, the magazine publishing business has been adversely affected by the economic climate of recent years.

Although it seems that the numbers have drastically improved from those of ten years ago, the fact remains that the magazine business can still be a volatile one. Results are not conclusive. However, it is important to understand some of the factors that can contribute to a magazine's failure or success, as these will also apply to digital. Know that a publication won't fail or succeed due to any one of the following reasons, but an examination of a few should indicate what kind of "health" your magazine is in. Refer to these often and make sure you are scoring higher on the side of success than on the side of failure.

Reasons for failure:

- Insufficient planning and research
- Insufficient budget and funds to cover magazine costs
- No clearly defined audience or target market
- Unfocused mission and editorial philosophy
- Inability to connect with readers
- The subject matter addresses a short-lived trend or fad that does not have an ongoing need for information
- Lack of effective marketing
- Inability to acquire significant distribution
- Unable to generate advertising income due to low circulation or poor visibility (without significant distribution)
- Bad design
- Unattractive covers and bylines that do not pull readers in
- Lackluster content
- Poor editorial direction
- Insufficient demand from consumers for the new publication
- Inexperienced management and staff

Reasons for success:

- Significant planning and research
- Sufficient funds to cover magazine costs until profits are expected
- A clearly defined audience and targeted market
- A highly focused mission and editorial philosophy
- A thorough understanding of audience wants and needs
- The magazine serves an ongoing need for information
- An effective marketing plan
- A distribution network that allows for high visibility
- Ability to attract advertisers and generate advertising income
- A great design that appeals to the intended audience
- Attractive covers and bylines that "force" readers to pick up and purchase—or subscribe to—the magazine
- Content that appeals to readers
- Great editorial direction
- High consumer demand
- Experienced management, staff, advisers, and freelancers

Chapter 2:
Planning Your Magazine

Is It Really a Magazine?

Before you begin this journey, it is important to answer the question of whether this is truly a magazine. While the subject matter may be of interest to you, how can determine that others will find it interesting also? How do you know that these particular information needs are not already being met elsewhere . . . online or otherwise? What will you do that is different? What unique perspective will you offer? And most importantly, how do you plan to engage your audience so that they might become loyal readers and subscribers?

Who are your readers? Do you have them defined? Is it a special niche audience? And if so, how do you plan to find them and make them aware of your new publication? How familiar are you with the market? What are their interests, problems, frustrations, concerns, dreams, aspirations, and fears? Are you an authority on the subject, or can you locate those who are? Is this a fad, or will readers have continuing information needs? Can you evolve editorially with each issue, or do you have enough information and ideas for just a few? Ultimately, is this really something people want to read about, will continue reading about, and why?

To help answer some of these questions, it is imperative that you study your competition. Check other magazines and magazine blogs that are similar to yours. Look at the way they are formatted and designed. Can you compete? Who currently advertises with them? How many subscribers do they have? What are their most popular topics? How often do they update their material? Check their social network accounts and see the number of followers there. Also, check the level of engagement, which will really give you an idea of how the subject matter is being received. While doing your research, pay special attention to the types of questions people ask or the requests they make to see if you notice any recurring patterns. This can provide clues as to what types of editorial opportunities exist and what content you may need to provide.

> **Tip:** To find the most popular magazines and blogs online, check Technorati (www.technorati.com). It provides the most comprehensive blog directory on the Web.

Next, hit Amazon.com and look at the customer reviews of competing or similar magazines. You can unearth a gold mine of information as you look at the comments to determine what a magazine is doing well and how it is satisfying its readers. Low-rated comments will also provide clues as to what you need to improve on to capture the attention of your desired audience. Build a long list of what your competitors do well (the pros) and not so well (the cons). This list can help you understand exactly what you need to do with your publication in the marketplace. Do not underestimate the tremendous amount of insight that can be gained from carrying out an exercise such as this.

All in all, do your homework and don't ignore the signs. You are about to invest a great deal of time into your project, so you need to know for sure that what "it" is is actually a magazine that there's a real audience for. Talk to peers, experts in the field, and special interest groups; go to chat rooms or social networks and post polls or surveys. Do anything you need to do to get significant feedback on your idea before you proceed.

Your Editorial Philosophy

After studying the competition, figuring out where you fit in, and determining that there is actually an audience for your magazine, it's time to create your editorial philosophy, which will act as the guiding light for your publication. When making various decisions concerning your magazine (even something as simple as deciding on the appropriateness of an article), you can always refer back to your philosophy and see whether it satisfies the criteria presented there.

To create an effective mission, you have to know exactly what your audience expects from your magazine and what you will do to satisfy those needs. It's imperative that you understand the function of your magazine in the life of your reader–after all, you'll be creating the publication for them. Your editorial philosophy should answer questions like:

- What is the magazine's main focus?
- What is the concept and purpose?
- What should it accomplish or achieve?
- Who is it aimed at?
- How is it different from other offerings in the marketplace?
- Why is there a need for its existence?
- What are the main areas of interest?
- What is the personality (voice or tone) of the publication?

EXAMPLE EDITORIAL PHILOSOPHY FOR A WOMEN'S MAGAZINE

MagazineXYZ is an inspirational magazine that instigates a woman's spiritual journey to inner strength, inner beauty, and inner peace. The main focus is affirmations, spirituality, self-improvement, and empowerment. The message will be delivered in a friendly, conversational tone, where readers will be able to say, "That is exactly what I was thinking and feeling, and that's the way I would have expressed it myself." This platform has been created for women to share their thoughts, feelings, and life experiences, providing them with a voice and a place where they can be heard, validated, and–ultimately–understood.

Your Editorial Formula

In determining your magazine's editorial formula, you will need to answer the following questions:

- What is the frequency of publication? (Weekly, monthly, etc.)
- Will you distribute your magazine for free, or will you require payment?
- If you plan to charge, how much will a single issue cost?
- How much will you charge for a subscription?
- How many issues of the magazine will a subscription cover?
- How many pages (or sections) will there be in each issue?
- How many pages will be allocated to editorial?
- How many pages for advertising?

- What will your advertising-to-editorial ratio be? (See tip below.)
- How many departments will there be?
- How many columns?
- How many features?

Although you may not be able to accurately fill in all the information at this time, you can "guesstimate" the figures based upon the research you have performed thus far and update them as you gain more knowledge as you continue to work through the upcoming chapters. It is important that you are familiar with the current conditions of the market, especially for your particular genre, so you can make an offering that is comparable to what already exists. Study other digital magazines. How much do they charge for subscriptions? What about per issue? How often do they publish? Find answers to the above questions based upon what is currently taking place in the marketplace and what you are capable of comfortably producing. See "Monetizing Your Magazine" in Chapter 11, in order to understand how to figure out your costs and how to compute the amount of advertising that will need to be sold in each issue to make your magazine profitable.

> **Tip:** According to a study on the advertising-to-editorial ratio conducted by Hall's Reports in 2012, print magazines carried 54.8 percent editorial vs. 45.2 percent advertising pages.

Just so you know, print magazines measure ad rates according to CPM (cost per thousand), which indicates the cost for an advertiser to reach 1,000 readers. It is calculated by dividing the page price by circulation. For instance, if your circulation is 5,000 and you charge $1,000 for a full-page ad, then your CPM = $1,000 / 5 = $200, meaning that it will cost an advertiser $200 to reach 1,000 readers. This term is also used for online marketing where CPM is the cost per 1,000 impressions. For example, a CPM of $1 would indicate a cost of $1 per 1,000 ad views.

Naming Your Magazine

Now that both your editorial philosophy and formula is in place and you're beginning to understand the direction of your magazine, it's time to give it a name. A magazine's name is one of its most important attributes, as it conveys the entire message to readers. It's the first thing someone will see or hear whether it's in conversation, as a search engine result, on the cover, or as the logo on your website. It's also a very important marketing tool that has to quickly communicate the right message to your audience.

Think of the qualities that you want your magazine to project and be identified with. Is the name descriptive? Is it easy to spell? Can readers pronounce it with ease? Is it memorable, or is it something that can easily be forgotten? And lastly, can it be visually made into a great logo and a website header?

Another consideration in name choice will be whether the domain name is available. You can check this at Go Daddy (www.godaddy.com). You should also check Facebook, Twitter, and other social networks to determine whether the name is available across the networks as well. To have consistency on all (which I highly recommend) you may have to opt for some type of variation of your originally thought-out name, or if you'd definitely like to keep the name, then you can create a slight variation that you only use across your social network accounts.

> **Tip:** Tweexchange (www.tweexchange.com) allows you to search both Twitter names and domain names (through Go Daddy) simultaneously. As you type a desired name into the search box, the site will display a side-by-side comparison of what's available and what's not for each. You may want to keep in mind that a Twitter username can be up to fifteen characters in length.

After you have narrowed your name choices down to a few, try them out on family and friends. Ask them what the name means to them and what image it conjures up. Find out if they can easily understand, pronounce, and spell it. Next, verify that you are not infringing on any copyrights or trademarks and that no one else is using the name by performing searches at both the U.S. Copyright Office (www.copyright. gov) and the U.S. Patent and Trademark Office (www.uspto.gov). You should also check with your local county clerk's office to see whether the name is already on the list of fictitious or assumed business names in your county. When you've followed all these steps and finalized your name choice, then I recommend that you register and claim it right away.

> **Note:** For more information on choosing and registering a domain, please see my top ten rules for selecting a domain name in Chapter 4 under "Choosing Your Host and Registering Your Domain."

Your Table of Contents

You've studied the competition, decided what subjects your audience will find most interesting, and figured out where you can fit in within the marketplace, so now it's time to demonstrate exactly how you plan to do that editorially. It is probably a good idea to follow the structure used by print magazines and think of your content in terms of departments (subjects that are grouped together under one common topic), columns (sections or articles that are usually written by an expert or a respected individual), and features (unique content that is neither a department nor a column but most clearly exhibits the magazine's philosophy).

Doing it this way will allow you to clearly arrange and organize your content offerings. Your table of contents will be vital in providing an overview of your magazine at one glance, so make sure to come up with clear, catchy, and descriptive titles that can draw readers in.

Don't start out with an intimidating list of items. Think about how much you and your team can realistically handle (maybe by focusing on what you consider to be the most important types of content first) and plan to grow from there. After you are actually published and available, you will then make contact with other contributors who will serve to flesh out your editorial offerings as your audience begins to grow.

Create your initial table of contents by starting with a description, deciding on a title, and then defining whether it will be a department or column. Feature stories can be decided upon and added once a particular theme for an issue has been selected.

EXAMPLE TABLE OF CONTENTS FOR AN ONLINE WOMEN'S MAGAZINE

Title	Description	Article Type
Shero	Featuring ordinary women doing extraordinary things	Department: For the Mind
The Queens of Conversation	Live commentary with six participants who discuss meaningful topics of interest	Department: For the Mind
Work It!	Picture-intensive fitness instructional guide	Department: For the Body
Your Health	Focusing on women's health	Department: For the Body
Soulfood	Affirmations (x2)	Department: For the Soul
Secret Confessions	Reader confessions page	Department: For the Soul
Chic Geek	High-tech gadget page	Column
Creating the Balance	Learning how to create utopia within	Column
Ask the Harpers	Down-to-earth relationship advice from a husband and wife team	Column

Your Editorial Calendar

An editorial calendar will allow you to strategically plan the publishing schedule and frequency of updates to your table of contents, whether publishing content to the Web or creating a digital magazine. What pieces are updated daily, biweekly, or monthly, etc.; on which days; and by whom? Your calendar should clearly outline this information. Remember, as far publishing articles to a website or blog, regularly and consistently updated material is key to your readers (and search engines) coming back for more. The less frequently you update, the fewer readers you will have.

Perform a search online for "editorial calendar template" to find a format that will work best for you. If creating a magazine blog and using WordPress, there is an editorial calendar plug-in that can help to schedule and manage content for multiple authors. (See Appendix A.) Use your calendar to let contributors know exactly when their content is due, so everyone is on the same page. I suggest that you always "pad" a date (add in extra days for time) in case of any unforeseen circumstances or complications. For instance, I might tell a writer that a story in due on the 9th of February, knowing that the actual due date might not be until a week later on the 16th. Also, allow time for editing, finding images, shooting video, or any other activity you may have to partake in before you consider the article as being complete and ready to go.

Think of the most convenient way you can share the calendar with contributors. A few options include Google Docs and Dropbox. But don't just post the calendar and forget about it. Regularly converse with your team to find out how everyone is doing and how things are coming along, whether by email, Skype, FaceTime, social network, text message, or otherwise. Aim to keep everybody up to date and informed.

Regardless of your publishing schedule, I suggest you map out the content for at least three to four issues of your magazine; you don't want to put all your effort into the first edition only to then realize that you have nothing left to say in subsequent issues. Having this information available will also be useful for your media kit so that advertisers can see where they can best align their products and services. Keep your calendar somewhat flexible to allow for breaking stories or news events that may arise. Bottom line, make sure your calendar is both workable and manageable without being at all overwhelming to you or your team.

Items you may want to track on your editorial calendar may include the following:

- Author's name
- Article title (or titles)
- Meta tag information (See Chapter 5.)
- Article description

- Article type (department, column, or feature)
- Category or section
- How often the section or page is updated (daily, weekly, biweekly, monthly, etc.)
- Additional content (images, video, podcasts, etc.)
- Draft due date
- Editor's name
- Edit due date
- Publication date
- Name of person responsible for publishing
- Additional notes

Note: Some of the items you track for publishing stories to a website or blog will not be necessary on the calendar of a digital publication and vice versa.

Chapter 3:
Finding Content and Images

Finding Content

WHERE TO FIND CONTENT

All publishers ask this question. Here are some possible resources:

Yourself: You must have something to write about; otherwise, you would have never come up with the idea of creating a digital magazine.

Your staff members or the people they know: Don't take this for granted. There's family, friends, and associates. Everyone knows an expert or someone with a great story to tell.

Your website: Post your writer's guidelines on your website for interested contributors.

Social media networks: Find experts, professionals, and writers specific to your particular genre by performing keyword searches on profiles or by joining groups that have a similar interest and connecting with individuals you find there.

Search engines: Pop a few terms that describe your particular subject matter into your favorite search engine and see what experts, websites, or blogs come up.

Specialized websites: Connect with journalists, bloggers, and other communications professionals at websites such as Helium (www.helium.com), Help A Reporter Out (www.helpareporter.com), and ProfNet from PR Newswire (www.prnewswire.com/profnet).

Freelance resources: To hire freelance writers, journalists, and bloggers, post requirements to sites such as Elance (www.elance.com), Freelancer (www.getafreelancer.com), and Guru (www.guru.com).

Reprints: These are previously published articles (either online, in print, or otherwise) that can be purchased for use within your own publication.

Free content available online: Some sites allow you to publish the articles found on their websites as long as you follow the guidelines as set out in the "terms of agreement." If you would rather not reprint the articles found there, then this is also a good way for you to find experts and specialists in your field. Such websites include Articlesbase (www.articlesbase.com), Articles Factory (www.articlesfactory.com), and EzineArticles (www.ezinearticles.com).

Organizations, associations, and special interest groups in your field: Find them online or offline in your area. Join social networking sites, chat rooms, discussion groups, newsgroups, and email lists to tell people all about your new publication and to publicize that you are looking for writers.

Universities and colleges: Find professors who are willing to share knowledge in their field of expertise.

Local journalism schools: Talk to educators, ask to use their most gifted students, and make arrangements for them to receive extra credit for their contributions.

Local writing clubs: Here you will find an abundance of eager writers who will be honored to contribute to your magazine.

Writing contests: This is a creative way of sourcing material.

Other newspapers and magazines (both online and offline): Scan these sources for story ideas or updates to previously published articles. Look for freelance writers who may post contact information along with their articles.

Classifieds: Advertise for writers either online (e.g., Craigslist) or offline (e.g., newspapers, writer's magazines, etc.).

WEBSITES FOR CONTENT IDEAS

Alexa (www.alexa.com)
Alexa, a subsidiary of Amazon, is the web information company that computes traffic rankings provided by the millions of Alexa toolbar users to provide you with the top 500 sites on the Web.

Alltop (www.alltop.com)
Alltop collects the headlines of the latest stories from the best websites and blogs that cover a specific topic. It then groups these collections, or aggregations, into individual web pages and displays the five most recent headlines from these information sources. Topics run from adoption to zoology, with stories about photography, food, science,

religion, celebrities, fashion, gaming, sports, politics, automobiles, and hundreds of other subjects in between.

BuzzFeed (www.buzzfeed.com)
BuzzFeed tracks the Web's obsessions in real time.

Digg (www.digg.com)
Digg is a place for people to discover and share content from anywhere on the Web, covering the latest headlines, videos, and images.

Engadget (www.engadget.com)
Engadget is a web magazine with daily coverage of everything new in gadgets and consumer electronics.

Google Alerts (www.google.com/alerts)
These are weekly, daily, or instantaneous alerts, sent to you via email, that contain the latest, most relevant Google results based on the keywords you select. Basically, the Google Alerts service allows you to create an automatic news finder.

Google News (news.google.com)
Google News is a computer-generated news site that aggregates headlines from more than 4,500 English-language news sources worldwide. Similar stories are then grouped together and displayed according to personalized interests.

Google Trends (www.google.com/trends/hottrends)
Google trends offers up-to-the-minute information on the hottest searches. It also allows you to compare the volume of searches between two or more terms.

Mashable (www.mashable.com)
Mashable reports on the importance of digital innovation and how it empowers and inspires people around the world.

Newsvine (www.newsvine.com)
Owned by MSNBC Interactive News (www.msnbc.com), Newsvine's purpose is "to build a perfectly different, perfectly efficient way to read, write, and interact with the news." Read stories from established media organizations as well as individual contributors from around the world.

popurls (www.popurls.com)
Known as the dashboard for the latest web buzz, it's a single page that encapsulates up-to-the-minute headlines from the most popular sites on the Internet.

reddit (www.reddit.com)
Touted as the voice of the Internet, it's like news before it happens.

Stuff to Tweet (www.stufftotweet.com)
Here you'll find the hottest topics featured on Digg, Delicious, Twitter, YouTube, Lifehacker, TMZ, Mashable, wikiHow, CNN, *The New York Times*, Dailymotion, Amazon, and Craigslist.

StumbleUpon (www.stumbleupon.com)
StumbleUpon helps you discover and share great websites, delivering high-quality pages that are matched to your personal preferences.

TechCrunch (www.techcrunch.com)
This media blog profiles start-ups, reviews new Internet products, and reports on breaking tech news.

Techmeme (www.techmeme.com)
This single, easy-to-scan page contains all the must-read tech stories.

Technorati (www.technorati.com)
Technorati is a blog directory covering numerous subjects and categories that also gives you the top 100 blogs of the day (www.technorati.com/blogs/top100).

Trendwatching.com (www.trendwatching.com)
This site features emerging consumer trends, insights, and related hands-on business ideas from around the world.

Working with Graphics and Images

UNDERSTANDING RESOLUTION

Resolution refers to how sharp an image is or appears. Images are described as being either low-resolution (low-res) or high-resolution (hi-res) files. Web graphics should be low-resolution, 72 dpi (dots per inch) files. Files of this size allow web pages to load quickly, an important usability factor on any website today. (To check an image's resolution in Photoshop, go to Image > Image Size.)

If creating a digital magazine, then I advise that you use high-resolution graphic files that have a minimum value of 300 dpi. Although using high-resolution files will result in larger files and longer download times, these images contain much more detail and information than low-resolution files, and can be enlarged or reduced without any loss of quality. They are perfectly suited for print purposes, which will be important if using HP MagCloud to create print editions of your magazine as will be discussed in Chapter 10. High-resolution files also allow users to zoom in on tablets and other devices and still receive clear, sharp (not blurry) images.

Using images of 150 dpi might somewhat allow for a happy medium, resulting in a smaller file size but sacrificing a little of the quality. If creating your flip book or app with an online vendor or service, the best thing to do is to check with them to see what their image requirements and recommendations are, as this can drastically impact the quality and download time of your publication.

USING STOCK PHOTOGRAPHY

To ensure you do not risk infringing on any existing copyrights, when not using original artwork it is best to acquire images from stock photography sites like those presented in the next section. Images found there will be licensed for specific purposes, so make sure you understand and follow the respective guidelines as presented on each site.

In general, there are two types of stock photography licenses available: royalty-free (RF) and rights-managed (RM). With a royalty-free license, you pay a flat fee that allows for unlimited use of a photo or illustration in any media as defined in the licensing agreement. On the other hand, a rights-managed photo is licensed for a one-time, specific use only. Fees are determined by the usage purpose which is defined according to numerous variables, including how the image will be used (publishing, brochure, advertising, etc.); whether it will be used on the cover, interior pages, or the Web; the size of the image on the page; expected length of time the image will be used; and so on and so forth. Using a rights-managed image can tend to be expensive and the terms rather limiting, so for convenience and flexibility—as well as affordability—I suggest you purchase royalty-free images.

WEBSITES FOR GRAPHICS AND IMAGES

Clip Art, Illustration, and Vector Images
www.clipart.com
www.illustrationworks.com
www.vectorstock.com

Free Photos (Low resolution)
www.flickr.com/creativecommons
www.freefoto.com
www.freephotosbank.com
www.morguefile.com

Free Photos (High resolution)
www.sxc.hu

Inexpensive Stock Photos (Low- and high-resolution files)
www.123rf.com
www.bigstockphoto.com
www.canstockphoto.com
www.crestock.com
www.dreamstime.com
us.fotolia.com
www.istockphoto.com
www.photoxpress.com

High-End and Subscription-Based Photo Sites (Low- and high-resolution files)
www.corbisimages.com
www.gettyimages.com
www.inmagine.com
www.punchstock.com
www.shutterstock.com
www.superstock.com
www.thinkstockphotos.com
www.wireimage.com

Chapter 4:
Your Online Presence

Choosing Your Host and Registering Your Domain

Your host's function is to store your website, or the pages you create, on its servers and display those pages over the Web. Your registrar is the company through which you will register your domain name. Your host and registrar can be one and the same, or they can be different; it's entirely up to you. If you decide to purchase a hosting plan from a provider that is different from your registrar, then your host will give you the instructions on how to "point" your domain to its servers so that you can physically host and administer your site with them. Either way, it's a quick and easy process to complete.

Over the years, I have built websites for clients using many different host providers, and the one I can highly recommend is Just Host (www.justhost.com). Their hosting plans start at around $3.75 per month, and the features offered just can't be beat. You get a free domain for life (so no extra cost is involved to register a new domain); unlimited website space (which means that if you need to upload a trillion videos, you can); unlimited streaming or data transfer; unlimited email accounts; free

WordPress, Joomla, and osCommerce installation; and worldwide 24/7 technical support that includes live chat. If that wasn't enough, there is also an anytime money-back guarantee. Just Host provides a simple, intuitive user interface (or control panel) that you use to administer your site. Also, when you purchase a plan, you receive unlimited domain hosting, which means you can host multiple domains on a single account. You'll never have to buy another hosting plan no matter how many websites you decide to create in the future.

If you are not ready to purchase a plan but would still like to secure your domain name, then I suggest registering at Go Daddy (www.godaddy. com). Hunt around for coupons online as the Internet is always rife with discount codes you can use for the service. Here are my eight rules for selecting a domain name:

- It should be a dot-com.
- It should be exactly the same name as your magazine. If that's not available, then choose something that's extremely close (maybe by popping "mag" onto the end for differentiation).
- It should be as descriptive as possible and provide a clue as to what your magazine is about.
- It should be reasonably short.
- It should be catchy, easy to remember, and easy to pronounce.
- It should not contain any underscores, as links are often highlighted or underlined, making a URL that contains an underscore somewhat hard to read.
- You should not use hyphens unless you absolutely have to, and even then, your address should not contain more than one. As in the case of a site called Who Represents (www.whorepresents.com), they might have been better off purchasing the hyphenated version so that the address would be much easier to decipher and read as www. who-represents.com.
- It should not be confusing or difficult to find (i.e., not the .net or .org name of an already existing, established, well-known .com site).

Pages, Sections, or Widgets Your Site Should Contain

Your website should be based on audience needs and set up in a way that makes it easy for visitors to browse and subscribe to your magazine. You should feature compelling, relevant, useful content that is updated regularly, as no one is going to return if you're featuring the same old boring content. Web communities are formed when users are entertained and engaged. Make it as interactive as possible by giving readers things to do. Supply content that encourages conversation and allows them to comment and provide feedback. You can also provide links from the content to a discussion board or social network so readers can connect, interact with one another (another important factor), and share ideas and information.

All magazines will have different requirements based on the format, subject matter, audience, style, and tone. However, at a minimum, the following pages, sections, or widgets should be included as part of your site.

Magazine Content Preview and Highlights

Display a sample of your magazine's content whether it be articles, video, podcasts, or other media. Make sure to feature and highlight links to your most popular content.

The Table of Contents (TOC)

If your magazine is web-based or in the form of a blog, then your website's navigation will serve as the TOC. Make your navigation clean, simple, intuitive, user friendly, and consistent throughout the site, clearly displaying all options that are available from the current location as well as highlighting exactly where a user is on the site so that there is no risk of ever getting lost or becoming confused. If your magazine takes another form of digital offering, such as a flip book or app, then feature your current TOC on the site where it is easy to access and view. Never force a user to download and open a file to look at your TOC.

Subscriptions

Create a simple sign-up form where readers can easily and conveniently subscribe online. Make the form prominent throughout your site.

Advertiser Page

Create a page specially dedicated to advertisers that provides direct contact information to your ad sales team, including names, phone numbers, email addresses, and links to social media accounts. Also, make sure to feature a downloadable PDF media kit (see next section).

About Us

Introduce your magazine, discussing your mission, concept, reason for being, or any other pertinent information that visitors may find interesting. Use language that gets them excited about your publication.

Newsletter Sign-Up Form

Create a space or page where readers can easily sign up to receive information via newsletter. This gives you the ability to collect email addresses and communicate directly with your audience. Keep them informed by sending out a monthly digest of your best content, relevant and interesting news, pertinent developments, information on events you may be holding, and any contests or special offers you may have. Your newsletter should contain enough interesting information that makes a reader want to click through to your site and further explore what's found there. Increase trust and your readers' willingness to divulge email information by including verbiage on the form similar to "This information will be used for correspondence only. We respect your privacy, and your email address will never be shared, sold, or rented." And of course, follow through with your promise. Also, remember to include an "opt-out" link in your newsletter as a courtesy should readers decide not to receive further emails. For email marketing services, you can check the following companies: AWeber (www.aweber.com), Constant Contact (www.constantcontact.com), iContact (www.icontact.com), and Mad Mimi (www.madmimi.com).

"Follow Us" Buttons

Provide links to all your active social network accounts. (The key word here is *active!*)

Social Media Sharing Buttons

Incorporate buttons that allow users to easily share your content with their personal networks on Facebook, Twitter, Digg, StumbleUpon, and others. AddThis (www.addthis.com) and ShareThis (www.sharethis.com) provide code, widgets, and plug-ins that allow you to add this feature to your site. Both services also provide analytic data that lets you see exactly where and how your content is being shared.

Contact Us

Provide a contact form where readers can send their comments, feedback, or inquiries. A contact form is a better choice because it protects your email address from exposure as opposed to a link, which can be easily picked up by "spam bots" and used to send spam mail.

Search Capability

Readers like having the ability to search for particular topics and information (possibly due to our Google habits), so don't miss out on providing this valuable tool on your site. Incorporating this function will also allow readers to search through and find articles from archived copies of your magazine.

Writer's Guidelines

Describe what types of articles you are looking for and exactly how they should be submitted. (See "Creating Your Writer's Guidelines" later on in the chapter.)

Ratings, Reviews, and Testimonials

Let visitors know all the good things people are saying about your magazine. Update these comments on a regular basis.

Survey

You can set up a survey to collect data on your readers that can be used to provide information to advertisers in your media kit. Gathering this information also allows you to tailor your website and magazine to satisfy audience needs. Add a disclaimer that lets readers know that their information will be kept confidential. It may read something akin to: "This information provides us with feedback so we can better serve your needs. All information provided will be kept confidential and not be disclosed or sold in any way." Zoomerang (www.zoomerang.com) is a free service that allows you to create web-based surveys that can be emailed out to recipients.

Note: Having a survey or questionnaire on your site, although valuable, may be considered the "old-fashioned" or outdated way of collecting information. With the advent of social media, you can now poll, question, and contact your audience in real time.

Ancillary Products

A publisher can sell products or services in addition to the magazine to raise awareness and generate additional income. Examples of such products or services include creating special industry reports; holding events, workshops, or seminars; selling books, videos, or training materials; or selling promotional items such as T-shirts, hats, and bags.

Games and Entertainment

Give your visitors something fun and relaxing to do. Get them "addicted" to your site by including additions such as horoscopes, polls, and quizzes. Aim to keep them hooked and coming back for more!

CREATING YOUR MEDIA KIT

Your media kit introduces your magazine to prospective advertisers and contains all the information they need to persuade them to place an ad with your magazine. It should make your prospect get interested in your publication, ultimately answering the question of why it's advantageous to advertise with you. Because of its importance, I suggest you have your media kit designed and laid out by a professional designer. It's true what they say: you never get a second chance to make a first impression. At a minimum, your media kit should contain the following:

A Compelling Cover

Make sure to create an enticing introductory page to your media kit.

Magazine Background and Information

Introduce your title. Who are you? What is your background? What qualifies you to publish a magazine in this field? What is your mission or editorial philosophy? Why is there a need for your magazine? How are you different from other publications in the marketplace?

Ratings, Reviews, and Testimonials

If you have or can generate some, add these to show advertisers the good things people are saying about the magazine.

Press Clips

Include any favorable media coverage or reviews you have received.

Reader Profile

Match the target audience with your advertisers. Provide demographic and psychographic information about them, answering questions like these: Who are my readers? What is their gender, age, family structure (number of children, extended family, etc.), geographic location, education level, profession or field, household income, and disposable income? What are their interests? What type of lifestyle do they lead? How do they spend their spare time? What motivates them? What are their Internet habits? What devices do they use? What types of purchases do they make? How often do they purchase products and services online?

The Number of Readers

Advertisers want to know that their message is reaching as many people as possible. Being a digital magazine, there are numerous ways you can choose to report this type of information, for example: the number of visitors to your site, magazine subscriptions, downloads, purchases, RSS subscriptions, email subscriptions, newsletter sign-ups, or the number of followers on your social networks. If you are a new magazine, then you may not be able to provide this information initially, but you will want to add this data as your magazine grows and significant numbers become available.

Market Analysis

Show why you have an attractive market by answering the following questions: What is the potential size of your target market? Is the market growing, and if so, due to what factors? What is the market growth rate? What makes the market profitable? What are the future trends for this market?

Editorial Calendar and Highlights

Give information about your content, showing the types of articles and themes that will be featured in upcoming months or throughout the year. This allows for advertiser tie-ins that enable advertisers to determine exactly when to advertise a particular product or service.

Rate Sheet

List your advertising rates and discounts here. The rate sheet summarizes a publisher's prices for ads of different sizes and positions; it also summarizes frequency discounts. In the example provided in Figure 1, you see the difference in price for purchasing one ad as opposed to the discounted rate given if (for instance) purchasing four.

Ad Sizes and Dimensions

Provide illustrations of the different ad sizes and dimensions that are available within the magazine. (See Figure 2.)

Figure 1: Media Kit - Example Advertising Rate Sheet for a Quarterly Magazine

Advertising Rates

Size	1x	2x	3x	4x
Full page	$1000	$ 900	$ 810	$ 730
2/3 page	$ 700	$ 630	$ 575	$ 540
1/2 page	$ 525	$ 480	$ 430	$ 400
1/3 page	$ 370	$ 330	$ 300	$ 270
1/6 page	$ 200	$ 180	$ 160	$ 140

Premium Positions

Cover 2 (inside front)	$ 1200
Cover 3 (inside back)	$ 1100
Cover 4 (back)	$ 1400
Inside Front Spread	$ 1600
Special Position Charge	$ 125

Marketplace

Marketplace (see dimensions and sizes)	$ 120

Send fifty words of copy, along with graphic(s) to marketplace@magazinexyz.com. Marketplace ads will be laid out in a standardized format. Please note: the marketplace ads section is subject to omission. If this occurs, a 1/6 page display ad will be substituted in its place.

PO BOX 12345, ATLANTA, GA 30003 • PHONE: 404.111.2222 • FAX: 404.111.2222 • EMAIL: ADS@MAGAZINEXYZ.COM
W W W . M A G A Z I N E X Y Z . C O M

Figure 2: Media Kit - Example Ad Sizes and Dimensions Page

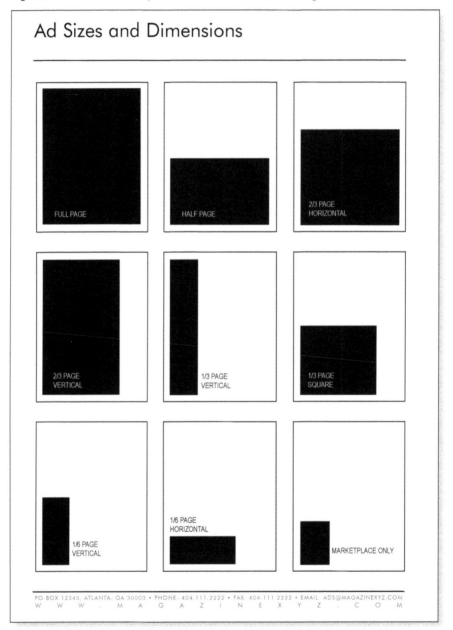

Figure 3: Media Kit - Example Advertising Reservation Form

Advertising Reservation Form

Company Name: _____

Contact Name: _____ Job Title: _____

Address: _____

City:_____ State:_____ Zip: _____ Web: _____

Phone: _____ Fax: _____ Email: _____

Type of Product(s) or Service(s) Advertised: _____

Reservation

Size	Ad Type?	Issue(s) in Which Ad Will Appear	Total No. of Ads	Total Due ($)

Payment

Payment Due Dates:

Winter 2014	October 15, 2014
Spring 2015	January 15, 2015
Summer 2015	April 15, 2015
Fall 2015	July 15, 2015

[ ] Check Enclosed [ ] MasterCard [ ] Visa Total Amount Enclosed ($) _____

Credit Card #:_____

Name on Credit Card: _____

Billing Address: _____

Rates are secure for all advertising orders that are contracted for a period of up to one year in advance.

Frequency discounts are contingent upon payment in full, for all ads in the series, by the payment due date for the first ad in the series.

Submission of this form to the Publisher constitutes agreement to the following terms and conditions. The Publisher reserves the right to reject or cancel any advertisement, space, position, or insertion order for any reason and at any time, previously accepted or not, without liability. The Publisher reserves the right to mark any advertisement "Paid Advertisement" or "Advertisement" if, in the judgment of the publisher, it looks like editorial content. Advertisers and advertising agencies assume liability for all content (including text, representations, and illustrations) of advertisements printed, and also assume responsibility for any claims arising therefrom. Acceptance of advertising does not relieve advertisers or agencies from liability. Advertiser shall receive the earned rate plus 10% for guaranteed premium placement on any insertion order; otherwise, placement cannot be guaranteed and is subject to revision up until the time of printing. If Advertiser fails to pay the rates indicated above or otherwise breaches this contract, the Publisher has the right to terminate this contract or modify the rate indicated above to the most current rate schedule plus 15%. Additional penalties may apply according to contract terms. Refunds are available for any cancellation made within one week after space reservation minus a $50.00 processing fee. Changes to ads are not accepted after the closing date. Ads received after the art submission deadline are subject to postponement.

The Publisher shall not be subject to any liability whatsoever for any failure to publish or circulate all or any part of any issue due to strikes, work stoppages, accidents, fires, acts of God, or any circumstance not within the control of the Publisher. The Publisher's liability for any error will not exceed the charge for the advertisement in question. The Publisher is not responsible for the accuracy of any corrections or changes made to any advertiser's materials. Rates are subject to change without notice. As used on this advertising reservation form, the term "Publisher" and "Magazine XYZ" refers to Magazine XYZ, LLC.

PLEASE RETURN THIS COMPLETED FORM TO:

_____
Signature

_____
Name (printed)

_____
Date

Magazine XYZ
Attention: Ad Sales Department
PO Box 12345
Atlanta, GA 30003
Office. 404.111.2222
Fax: 404.111.2222
Email: ads@magazinexyz.com
Website: www.magazinexyz.com

PO BOX 12345, ATLANTA, GA 30003 • PHONE: 404.111.2222 • FAX: 404.111.2222 • EMAIL: ADS@MAGAZINEXYZ.COM
W   W   W   .   M   A   G   A   Z   I   N   E   X   Y   Z   .   C   O   M

Submission Requirements

Let advertisers know what file types will be accepted for ad submission. Examples include PSD, AI, PDF, JPEG, TIFF, MP4, AVI, MOV, MP3, AIFF, and WAV.

Deadlines

List the space reservation, ad file submission, and payment due dates.

Advertising Reservation Form

Create an advertising order form that outlines the specifics and details of an ad. (See Figure 3.) A web form could also be set up to accept this information along with payment.

Staff and Contributor Bios

If it helps to make your magazine look more credible, list some of the main profiles here.

Business Address and Sales Contact Information

Let advertisers know where, how, and whom to contact; you'd be surprised how many people forget to include this vital information.

CREATING YOUR WRITER'S GUIDELINES

Your writer's guidelines describe exactly what you are looking for in articles to be considered for publication. Visit FreelanceWriting (www.freelancewriting.com) where you will find a database with links to over eight hundred writer's guidelines from magazines that span more than fifty-six different subject categories. At a minimum, your guidelines should include the following:

An introduction to your magazine

EXAMPLE: Thank you for your interest in writing for *MagazineXYZ*. *MagazineXYZ* covers all aspects of a woman's life, featuring personal, first-person stories. Dubbed as "a manual for women who want to make better choices," *MagazineXYZ* aims to feed the soul, encourage, motivate, and inspire.

Description of the editorial style, voice, and tone of the magazine

EXAMPLE: The editorial voice of submitted works should be friendly, intimate, relaxed, conversational, and very down to earth–just as if you were sitting around chatting with a bunch of friends. Where appropriate, please feel free to inject as much of your personality, personal values, and thoughts into the article as possible. This is your article from your point of view, so give people a taste of who you are, how you are feeling, and exactly what you think.

Article length and expectations

EXAMPLE: Although we do not like to give a required length (as we feel that the content of a particular article should dictate its length), we would suggest that submissions be no longer than 1,000 words, with the ideal range being between 500–700 words. Please concentrate more on quality and making sure the information is both engaging and easily digestible by readers than on word count. Because you are writing for a digital magazine, articles should be somewhat "scannable." To ensure review of your materials, please only submit final drafts of your work as we have limited editorial staff and cannot spend time editing submissions.

Directions on exactly how articles should be submitted

EXAMPLE: Submit articles and story pitches (an idea for an article) via email to *articles@MagazineXYZ.com*. Put the words "Editorial Submissions" in the subject line and indicate the article category. We accept MS Word, TXT, and HTML files as well as GIF, JPEG, PSD, AI, and TIFF picture files. If your work is in a format other than the aforementioned, please send the text of your query or submission in plain text in the body of your email to ensure that we can read the format of your file. We also accept the following video and audio file formats: MP4, AVI, MOV, MP3, AIFF, and WAV.

Information authors should provide

EXAMPLE: Please include your name, email address, and cell phone number. If this is your first time submitting to us, please tell us about yourself, including your experience, background, and qualifications for submitting a particular story. If you have any previously published clips, please include a representative sampling of no more than three items, please.

What authors can expect after submitting a story

EXAMPLE: We do our best to respond to all inquiries, but be aware that we are sometimes inundated. If your writing sample (or other submission) meets our requirements, then a staff member will contact you. Allow at least two months for a response. If you have not heard back from us within this period, please assume that we will not be able to use your idea or submission at this time.

The topics you are interested in receiving

EXAMPLE: *MagazineXYZ* is interested in receiving submissions on a variety of topics, including (but not limited to) the following:

- Emotional, spiritual, or physical well-being
- Motivational and inspirational pieces
- Personal experiences, true stories, and confessions
- Love, sex, and relationships
- Political or social issues
- Entertainment news
- Book, music, film, or video reviews

- Events coverage
- Hair and beauty
- Fashion
- Health and fitness
- "How to" -type stories (e.g., how to start your own business, how to fix your credit, etc.)
- Family
- Business advice
- Money and finance
- Home décor and gardening tips
- Food and recipes
- Travel
- Subjects from the male perspective
- Humor

Compensation offered

EXAMPLE: Pay rate is discussed on an individual basis and determined by the type of article submitted as well as the relevant experience of a writer.

Submitting Your Site to Search Engines

We have all seen the "We will submit your site to 75,000-plus search engines and directories for the low price of $29.95!" offers. But come on now, think about it. What 75,000 search engines and directories do you know of that exist? At most, I can recall about five, and evidently they are the only five I really need to know. So even if this claim is true, it is definitely overkill!

These days, search engines are so good at finding and indexing websites that it is no longer necessary for you to do the process yourself by manual submission or through a service. Diehards and control freaks like me, and especially those who have a new site under a new domain name, should visit Free Web Submission (www.freewebsubmission.com), where you will find direct links to the top fifty highest ranked search engines and directories that you can submit your site to. It can take up to two weeks before you see your site show up in search results. If you wish to carry out the submission process yourself, then submitting to the following three will suffice:

Bing (www.bing.com/toolbox/submit-site-url)
Dmoz (www.dmoz.org)
Google (www.google.com/addurl)

Note: Yahoo! submissions now take place through Bing, so submitting your site to Bing means that you are submitting to both.

Monitoring Your Site with Google Analytics

After your site is showing in listings and has been up and running for a few months, it's a good idea to check your web statistics to determine how well your site is performing by analyzing how visitors are interacting with it. Google Analytics is the most popular and widely used tool for this purpose, providing statistical data in the form of graphs and reports you can use to gauge site performance. On signing up for an account (accounts. google.com) and registering your site, you will be provided with a tiny snippet of JavaScript code that will need to be installed across all pages so that you can track relevant statistics. If using a content management system such as WordPress, then you will need to add the code (once) directly into your template or theme. Alternatively, you may use the Google Analytics for WordPress plug-in.

Monitoring site statistics will give you insight into what works and what doesn't so that you might improve your content offerings, site design, features and functionality, marketing initiatives, or keyword selections. (See "Keyword Research Strategies" in Chapter 5.) This information will also help you decide what activities you need to continue focusing on, increase, or possibly eliminate altogether. Find out who visits your site, from where, when, what search terms were used, how long visitors stayed, what path they took, what pages were most popular, and what pages your site was most commonly exited from. In particular, pay attention to the following statistics:

Traffic Sources

Find out the top sources of traffic to your site so that you can measure the effectiveness of your marketing activities. What websites are regularly sending traffic your way? Are most visitors coming to you via search engine or via social network? Which ones in particular? Monitoring this stat will provide you with the answer.

Keywords

This statistic monitors the keyword phrases or terms visitors used to search for and find your site. Look at these results to determine whether your targeted keywords are accurate and pages delivered matched the information visitors were looking for. High bounce rates for a term (which occur when a visitor leaves a site after viewing a single page) can indicate that the page was not relevant and did not meet expectations. This statistic can also provide hints as to what additional content you may need to provide.

Total Visitors

This statistic lets you see how many different people visited your website within a fixed time frame, usually hourly, daily, weekly, or monthly. If the same visitor visits your site on January 1st and then again on January 3rd, then that visitor would be counted twice as a daily unique visitor and once as a weekly or monthly unique visitor.

New vs. Returning Visitors
If there are a high number of new visitors to your site, then you can determine that you are being successful in driving traffic to your site. If there are a high number of return visits, then you can determine that readers are finding your content engaging, relevant, and useful.

Mobile
This shows the number of visits that came from a mobile device (including tablets) and what those devices were (e.g.,Apple iPad, Apple iPhone, Samsung Galaxy, HTC Sapphire).

Page Views (or Unique Page Views)
This shows which pages are most popular on your site, indicating what readers are finding most valuable or entertaining. This statistic can be used to see whether changes to certain pages result in more visits or what kind of content you need to provide to keep visitors engaged.

Click Path or Visitor Path
This statistic shows the sequence of hyperlinks followed or the actual path a visitor took while browsing through a website. Following this statistic can help you understand why visitors come to your site and what they look for after they get there.

Landing Pages
Landing pages are the most popular pages upon which visitors enter a site. The more relevant the page, the less likely a visitor will be to bounce or leave right away. If you notice high bounce rates on certain pages, try to analyze why (i.e., determine what source the traffic came from or what keywords were used) and assess what functionality or content you need to add or change to satisfy expectations.

Exit Pages
This statistic shows the last page a reader visited before leaving your site. If you notice a high dropout rate on a certain page, then you

may consider updating the content or simplifying the design. Although results are not conclusive, this statistic, when used in conjunction with the click path or visitor path, may reveal what pages users find least useful, boring, or confusing.

Visit Duration

This statistic shows how long visitors spent on your site (in increments of seconds) and how many pages they viewed in that time. Depending on the type or function of your website, you will have different ideal targets for this statistic.

Conversions

A conversion is defined as the number of visitors who complete a desired action beyond just surfing and perusing your site. Desired actions could be purchasing a subscription, signing up for a newsletter, or downloading a file. This statistic, when set for the particular action you would like to measure, allows you to determine just how well your site is fulfilling its business goals.

Using Social Media Listening Tools

Social media listening tools allow you to search, track, and analyze conversations that are happening on the Web in real time. This can be extremely valuable in finding out who's talking about you (or your competitors) and exactly what they're saying . . . good, bad, or indifferent. Here are some ideas of what you should be listening for on the networks:

Your magazine's name: Who's talking about you? What are they saying? How are you generally being perceived in the market? On what social networks or sources (blog, news site, etc.) are you being talked about? Who and where are your advocates and key influencers? Whenever possible, actively respond to readers and thank them for their comments and interest. If what readers say is not that positive and you feel their comments warrant a response, then acknowledge the feedback by thanking them for their input and for bringing their concerns to your attention. Let them know that you are always looking for ways to improve your publication and that this is something you will be working on in the future. Some folks may just be acting plain old mean. They are called Internet trolls. It may be best to ignore them, but otherwise learn to use negative comments in a positive way.

Your URL: When monitoring your URL, do not add "www" to your search query, as most people will simply leave that part off. Find out who's directing folks to your website by sharing your URL and why.

The central topic(s) upon which your magazine is based: Keep up to date on the buzz of what's happening in your industry so that you can effectively respond, participate, and be in the know. Staying current is extremely important for a digital magazine. You can plan editorial content around breaking or developing news. Better yet, if you're the one who's breaking the news and creating the buzz. Use this technique to find potential readers for your magazine by setting up queries for your most important keyword phrases and seeing who's having conversations on the topic. Depending on the network being used, you may have the ability to chime in right away. If you think an article or a section of your magazine could be of value, then make the user aware of it and point them in that direction. You should be an expert on your subject matter and have the ability to strike up conversations regarding the specific information, possibly letting them know that you currently work for "X" magazine and feature that type of content on your website and throughout your publication.

The names of competing or similar magazines: Track both the names and URLs of other magazines in your genre. Although you've already researched these magazines, you'll want to keep abreast of their latest developments, which includes staying on top of how their audience continues to respond to them.

The digital magazine industry as a whole: It is important to stay updated on the latest trends within the industry, as the field (much like everything else that is happening on the Internet) is in constant flux. What innovations are taking place with other digital magazines? Who are the latest successes (or failures) and why? What new software solutions or services are being developed that can help you streamline your process and create a better product? Monitoring the industry in general will provide you with these answers. (See Appendix B "Industry News and Resources.")

SOCIAL MEDIA LISTENING TOOLS

There are numerous tools and services that can perform the function of social media listening. Find a list here of the more popular free tools available. As will be indicated, some of the sites also provide a more robust paid version of their services.

Addict-o-matic (www.addictomatic.com)
Addict-o-matic pulls the latest news, blog posts, videos, and images from selections of sites, such as Google, Bing, YouTube, Flickr, Technorati, WordPress, Newsvine, and Digg. Results appear on a single page, grouped together in boxes according to the originating source. Bookmarking the results of a specific search allows you to receive the most recent updates whenever you access the page using the saved bookmark.

Google Alerts (www.google.com/alerts)
As previously mentioned in Chapter 2's "Websites for Content Ideas," Google Alerts can be set for weekly, daily, or instantaneous alerts on the subjects of your choice. Results consist of Google search results and are sent directly to your email.

Figure 4: Social Mention Search Sources

socialmention*

Real-time social media search and analysis:

			in	All
or select social media sources				All
ask	backtype	bbc	bebo	Blogs
bleeper	blinkx	blip	blogcatal	Microblogs
bloggy	bloglines	blogmarks	blogpulse	Networks
boardtracker	break	clipmarks	clipta	Bookmarks
dailymotion	delicious	deviantart	digg	Comments
facebook	faves	flickr	fotki	Events
friendster	google blog	google buzz	google ne	Images
highfive	identica	iterend	jumptags	News
lareta	linkedin	metacafe	msn socia	Videos
mybloglog	myspace	myspace blog	myspace	Audio
netvibes	newsvine	ning	omgili	Questions
photobucket	picasaweb	pixsy	plurk	
reddit	samepoint	slideshare	smugmug	spnbabble
stumbleupon	techmeme	tweetphoto	twine	twitarmy
twitpic	twitter	twitxr	webshots	wikio
wordpress	yahoo	yahoo news	youare	youtube
zooomr				

Hootsuite (www.hootsuite.com)

Hootsuite is a social media management system (not just a listening tool) that allows you to manage and post to multiple networks such as Twitter, Facebook, LinkedIn, Foursquare, Google+, MySpace, and WordPress through a secure, web-based dashboard. You can schedule posts, upload images, shorten URLs, and create custom reports using the comprehensive set of social analytic measurement tools provided. The listening portion of the tool allows you to search Twitter for mentions, keywords, and hashtags. Hootsuite comes in both free and paid versions, with the free version allowing you to register and administer up to five social media accounts.

Figure 5: Topsy Comparison Search

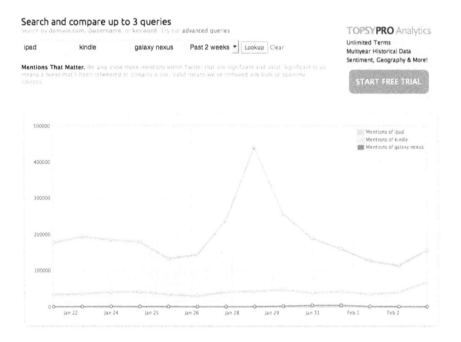

Monitter (www.monitter.com)

Monitter is a real-time tool that functions much like a stock ticker and lets you monitor location-specific (if required) Twitter conversations for particular words and hashtags. The scrolling results window displays each user's image along with the tweet that matches your set criteria. You can simultaneously view the streams of several subjects at a time, as results appear next to one another in column format.

Social Mention (www.socialmention.com)

Social Mention is an easy-to-use search and analysis tool that aggregates content from a wide range of sources around the Web into a single stream of information. You can select to restrict results to certain social networks or, for example, to only query microblogs. (See Figure 4.) Social Mention also produces statistics on your search that include sentiment (whether the responses were positive, negative, or neutral), top keywords, top users, passion (the frequency of mentions by the same authors), and sources. Results can be saved as .CSV Excel files, email alerts can be triggered, or you can choose to set up an RSS feed.

Topsy (www.topsy.com)
Topsy currently offers two products on its website, namely Social Search and Social Analytics. Social Search gives real-time insight into relevant conversations that are taking place on the Web. Unlike the other tools, Topsy uses an algorithm that indexes and ranks results based upon the most influential conversations it finds on the Web. The advanced search lets you drill down enough to construct very specific terms that can be found within a site, domain, or a particular Twitter user's stream. The Social Analytics portion allows you to search and compare up to three queries at a time (for instance, the iPad, Kindle, and Galaxy Nexus as shown in Figure 5). A graph shows all the Twitter mentions received over a given time period, and a table is presented with three tabs that contain the links to mentions received in the last twenty-four hours. Topsy comes in both free and paid versions.

WhoTalking (www.whotalking.com)
This real-time social media topic search engine lets you search for conversations on sites such as Twitter, Facebook, Google+, YouTube, Flickr, Picasa, and Digg.

Understanding RSS

RSS stands for "Really Simple Syndication," and it allows you to syndicate content to a subscriber who is automatically notified every time you add new content to your blog, website, or podcast series.

The information is delivered directly to a subscriber without the need to bypass any filters (as with email marketing) and displayed through an RSS reader, also known as a "news aggregator" for text and a "podcatcher" for podcasts. RSS readers can be web-, desktop-, or mobile device-based.

The most popular readers can be found at Google Reader (www.google.com/reader) and through My Yahoo!. The latest versions of Internet Explorer and Safari have RSS readers built in, as does Firefox, which incorporates a live bookmarks feature. RSS readers function somewhat like email with the list of unread feeds, or headings, from all the subscribed-to websites aggregately displayed in one place. When you click on an entry, you can see, read, or hear the latest updates from right there in the window, or you can choose to click through to the selected site.

Give interested visitors a way to subscribe, stay updated, and become loyal readers without the need to even have to visit your site. Note that it is important to measure the number of RSS subscriptions or podcast downloads because these readers will not be able to be tracked by Google Analytics, as they are not actually visiting your site to view content. By syndicating content, you will generate a ton of backlinks to your site and search engines just love backlinks. Having an RSS feed also increases your blog's visibility because now you can send your content directly to news aggregators such as Yahoo! and Google.

Figure 6: RSS Icon

Sites that offer subscriptions have a little RSS icon (usually orange in color) placed somewhere on the page. An RSS icon may also be displayed to the right of a URL in the browser window's address bar. To subscribe to a feed, simply click on the icon and follow the instructions presented.

RSS TOOLS

Most blogging software automatically creates an RSS feed for you, so all you may have to do is simply turn the feature on and forget about it. If your software does not provide this automatic RSS function, then you can try one of the services listed below. I have also included Feed Validator, so you can ensure that your RSS output (or XML code) has been generated without errors.

FeedBlitz (www.feedblitz.com)
This is an email marketing service for blogs, social media, and RSS.

FeedForAll (www.feedforall.com)
Easily create, edit, and publish RSS feeds and podcasts (including iTunes-compatible podcasts) with desktop software. Note that FeedForAll is available for Mac OS X only.

Feed Validator (www.feedvalidator.org)
This ensures that there are no problems with your feed. Any errors found will be highlighted, and the appropriate correction message(s) will be given.

Google FeedBurner (www.feedburner.com)
This online feed creation and management service is compatible with several popular blog engines and provides statistical information, such as how many subscribers you have and what articles are most popular on your site. Feed updates can be automatically delivered by web portal, news reader, or email.

Twitterfeed (www.twitterfeed.com)
Twitterfeed feeds your blog directly to Twitter, Facebook, LinkedIn, and various other networks.

PING YOUR WEBSITE OR BLOG

After you have RSS set up and you are regularly updating your site, then it will be necessary for you to ping your website or blog. Pinging allows you to immediately notify search engines, directories, and other services every time new, updated content appears on your site. When a site receives your ping in the form of the newly generated URL, it enters a queue for indexing and addition to the site. Although most blogging software automatically pings a selected set of services, you may want to take an extra few minutes to help improve visibility and the speed at which search engines will index your site by performing a manual ping using one or two of the free services listed below. Just so you know, Ping-O-Matic is the most popular of these tools.

> Autopinger (www.autopinger.com)
> BlogBuzzer (www.blogbuzzer.com)
> Feed Shark (feedshark.brainbliss.com)
> Google Blog Search Ping Service (blogsearch.google.com/ping)
> Pingates (www.pingates.com)
> Ping-O-Matic (www.pingomatic.com)

Chapter 5:
Preparing Search Engine-Friendly Web Pages

Understanding SEO

Search engine optimization (SEO) is the official term for improving the visibility, or rankings, of a web page in search engine results. Search engines work by sending out automated programs, called spiders or robots, that crawl the Internet, visiting sites, reading the information found there, and then indexing this information by storing the results in a database. Crawlers refresh these indexes at different intervals, periodically returning to sites to check for updated content. Storing the data this way allows for quick searches online; otherwise, bots would have to physically crawl the Internet every time a search is performed. I couldn't even begin to imagine how long a method like that would take today.

Considering that 80 percent of traffic to a website comes through a search engine, it is imperative that as a digital magazine publisher, you understand the principles presented in this chapter. Making your website search engine friendly simply means that a web page has been coded in a way that makes it easily accessible to these crawlers, explicitly and clearly providing the specific information they look for as well as presenting that information in the best possible manner. There are two primary methods used by search engines for finding, indexing, and cataloging your site:

1. Keywords, which allow each page on your website to be relevant for particular search terms
2. Meta tags, which are special HTML tags that provide information about the contents of a web page, as explained in "Placing Keywords within HTML Meta and Header Tags" later on in the chapter

KEYWORD RESEARCH STRATEGIES

Your job is to find the most common phrases used to search for your particular subject matter and include those terms as keywords on your web pages so that you might rank higher in search results for those terms, thereby increasing your chances of actually being found on the Web. When creating your list of keywords, try not to be too general. Remember, you are competing against a ton of other websites out there, so it's important that you zone in on specific search terms and phrases.

Never use one-word keywords, as this will guarantee that you don't get high rankings. For instance, if your magazine focuses on the subject of golf, don't just use the word "golf" or "golfing" as a keyword. Instead, use phrases such as "perfecting your golf swing," "how to align a golf shot," "golf swing training," or "free golf instruction guides."

When researching the best keywords to use for your particular niche, take "long tail keywords" into consideration. Long tail keywords consist of three or more words that are the less common, less competitive keywords searched for but that can be responsible for delivering significant levels of high-quality, targeted traffic to a site. For instance, the specific phrase "Canon PowerShot Digital Camera," as opposed to the more general "digital camera," indicates that the searcher knows exactly what he or she is looking for and is probably ready to take some type of action, whether that means making a purchase, signing up for a newsletter, or downloading a report. Focusing on less popular terms can also increase your site's chances of being highly ranked for your selected keyword phrases.

To clearly define what your audience searches for—just as you did when planning your magazine and researching the competition—spend some time browsing the Web, visiting similar sites and their corresponding social networks. Take note of the types of problems discussed and the kinds of words and phrases used, making sure to jot down any recurring themes you find. Plug these phrases into a keyword research tool to see what other keywords or phrases you can come up with. Cross-check your results by repeating the exercise in at least one other tool to see if you can generate any more options. If using Google AdWords, you can also plug your URL—or a competitor's URL—into the website field for a list of suggested keywords. Compile a list of keyword phrases that you find that are not too competitive and appear most consistently across results.

KEYWORD RESEARCH TOOLS

Free Services
Google AdWords (https://adwords.google.com)
SEMRush (de.semrush.com)

Paid Services with Free Trials
Keyword Discovery (www.keyworddiscovery.com)
Wordtracker (www.wordtracker.com)

To go into more depth regarding the actual keywords that a competing site is using, enter any of the keyword phrases from the list you have now compiled into your favorite search engine and note the sites that show up in the top set of results that closely match your content offerings. Head over to ABAKUS Topword (www.abakus-Internet-marketing.de/tools/ topword.htm) and enter each of the URLs you have found there.

This amazing tool analyzes the top keywords in a web page, providing you with a list of the most used single keywords, two-word phrases, and three-word phrases that can be found on a page. Once again, look for similarities and differences between these results and what you have already found. Using the information you have already compiled, create a final master keyword list that consists of at least six to ten phrases you can use as target phrases on various pages or articles throughout your site.

It is important to know that search engines read web pages from the top down. Aim to place your keyword phrases at the very top of the page (if you can, before the main header or navigation), and toward the front of the first set of paragraphs. (Think headline, headline, headline; and yes, subheads too.) Continue to sprinkle your phrases throughout the content or text on your page.

The main pages of your site should be optimized for at least one specific search term, with your home page being optimized for your most important keyword phrase. This strategy allows the pages in your site to rank for several keyword terms (instead of just one), and it also eliminates the possibility of pages within your site competing against one another for particular search terms.

Always ensure that your content is packed with information in a way that makes it relevant, unique, interesting, and useful to a visitor. Don't try to stuff so many keywords in that your content becomes nonsensical. Although you're aiming to make your pages search engine friendly, your first order of business is to ensure your page is readable and makes complete sense to your readers. If they are unable to make heads or tails out of what they're reading, then they won't be visitors for long. Attempting to overstuff content with keyword phrases (and other questionable SEO tactics, such as attempting to hide keywords by making your text color the same as the color of your background) is known as "black hat search engine optimization," and is generally frowned upon by most search engines.

PLACING KEYWORDS WITHIN HTML META AND HEADER TAGS

Now we're about to get technical! Although these actions may be performed by your web designer, it is important that you understand this information for the following reasons:

1. To ensure that either you or your designer knows about and is actually building web pages that are coded correctly for search engine spiders
2. To ensure that you can have an intelligible conversation (with your designer or another party) regarding the subject matter
3. To ensure that you create effective, appropriate "titles" and "meta tags" for the web pages on your site
4. To ensure that you apply these principles to ALL online marketing activities you may perform from creating articles, newsletters, podcasts, or videos to performing social media marketing activities

Grab a pen or pencil and go line by line through the HTML code in Figure 7 until you truly understand what is going on. Depending on your knowledge level (we all have to start somewhere), it may be necessary for you to read this section over a few times. Have patience. I promise that if you take it slowly, you will eventually get it. So here goes . . .

HTML is a computer language that defines the structure and layout of a web page on the Internet. This language tells your browser how to display words and images on a web page by using code that contains a variety of "tags" and "attributes."

Tags are HTML commands that provide instructions to a browser. They usually come in pairs like <p> and </p>, where the first tag is called an opening tag and the second (that always includes a backslash) a closing tag. Just so you know, the **<p>** tag tells a browser to start or open a new paragraph, and the **</p>** tag tells the browser to close it.

An attribute allows you to further specify the particular characteristic of a certain tag. For a real-world example, if a tag were a dress suit, then the attributes could be blue color, wool fabric, medium size, and gold buttons. This is about as technical as you will need to get, and the clarification of these terms will become more apparent as we progress through this section.

Imagine you saw the following information displayed on a web page in a browser window:

Imagine the word red being red, green being green, and blue being blue. Figure 7 presents the HTML code that has been used to construct the page. You will see the attributes used to create the different colored text as well as the bold, italicized, and small type that appears on the page.

Starting at the top, the "**DOCTYPE**" declaration is always the first instruction that appears in an HTML document. It tells your browser what particular version of the markup language the page is written in.

Figure 7: HTML Code

```
<!DOCTYPE html PUBLIC "-//W3C//DTD XHTML 1.0
      Transitional//EN" "http://www.w3.org/TR/
      xhtml1/DTD/xhtml1-transitional.dtd">
<html xmlns="http://www.w3.org/1999/xhtml">

<head>
  <meta http-equiv="Content-Type" content="text/html;
      charset=UTF-8"/>
  <title>Publish Your First Digital Magazine by
      Lorraine Phillips
  </title>

  <meta name="description" content="Find ideas,
      strategies, tools and solutions you can use to
      create a digital publication.">
  <meta name="keywords" content="" >
  <meta name="author" content="Lorraine Phillips" >
</head>

<body>
    <h1>Keyword Rich Article Title</h1>

    <h2>Subhead with Related Keywords</h2>
        <p>Pages should be information AND keyword
           rich, specially designed to contain the
           most popular, most likely keywords that
           people will use to search for the content
           that is found on your site online.
        </p>

    <h3>Another Subhead with More Keywords</h3>
        <p>Text can be displayed in numerous styles
           including <strong>bold</strong>,
           <em>italicized</em>, or <font size=-1>
           small</font>. Text can also appear in
           various colors such as <font color="red">
           red, </font> <font color="green">green,
           </font>or <font color="blue">blue</font>.
        </p>

</body>
</html>
```

The "**html xmlns**" statement tells the browser what language standards have been implemented on the page, and in our case, these standards can be found at www.w3.org/1999/xhtml.

The information contained within the "**head**" tags (**<head>** opens the tag, and **</head>** closes it) provides important information that is used by search engines to catalog and index your site. Note that the information contained within this tag is not actually displayed on the page by the browser.

Skipping to the "**title**" tag, it reads, "Publish Your First Digital Magazine by Lorraine Phillips." This tag is extremely important. Search engines use this tag as one of the primary means for cataloging your site so you should aim to include your most significant keywords here according to the content that will be found on the page. When someone does an online search and your site is returned in the results, this will be the text of the clickable link that is presented. Make it descriptive, informative, and inviting so that your link is the one that gets clicked, as opposed to the others that appear in the list. As you can see, the information contained within the title tag is displayed at the top of the browser window when a user actually visits the page, and it is also the text used if a visitor bookmarks the page or adds it as a favorite. The title tag should be unique for every page on your site and fewer than 70 characters in length.

The next set of tags within the head are called "**meta tags**." We can ignore the "**keywords**" attribute because due to abuse, this is no longer used by major search engines, such as Google and Yahoo!, to categorize a site. The "**description**" attribute includes a brief one- or two-sentence description of the page and is the text that will be displayed underneath the clickable link in search results. This description—if well written, concise, and informative—should assist with click-through rates to your site, as the verbiage you present here should help searchers quickly determine whether the page contains the information they are looking for. To avoid signs of keyword stuffing, DO NOT use the same keywords as found in your title tag. Aim to vary the description presented for each page on your site by providing a brief summary of the content that appears there.

To avoid being truncated in returned search results, make the description approximately 150 characters in length, including spaces. Moving on to the "**author**" tag, the tag is not required but can help with name recognition for your magazine, so enter your magazine's name here.

Continuing on with our example, the "**body**" tag defines all the contents that will actually be displayed by the browser, such as text, hyperlinks, images, videos, tables, and lists; describing not only the what but also the how. Pages should be information AND keyword rich, specially designed to contain the most popular, most likely keywords that people will use to search for the content that is found on your site.

The H1 thru H6 tags are known as "**header**" tags (not to be confused with the previously discussed "head" tag) and used to define HTML headings on a web page. H1 is used to define your most important heading, while H6 defines the least important one. **<h1>** should be used for your article title or headline, placed at the beginning of an article (don't try to be snazzy), and contain your main keywords. Because of the importance and prominence of the information contained within the H1 tag, using this tag accurately can provide you with a significant rankings boost in search engine results. Subsequent H2 to H6 tags should be used for subheadings as needed to further break down the elements of your topic-centered page, and they should contain different keyword phrases.

When using keywords, you should also consider keyword proximity. Keyword proximity refers to the closeness between two or more keywords, with the general consensus being the closer the keywords, the better the results. For instance, "IT support services for small business" would be more effective than "We provide IT support services and only work strictly with small businesses." When at all possible, avoid using filler words between phrases.

As a general rule of thumb, your keyword phrases should be no more than 7 percent of the total number of words presented on a page. If there are more than that, then you risk appearing as a keyword spammer to search engines, which can result in your page being penalized or even totally excluded from results.

Understand that there is no magic bullet or formula that can catapult your site to the top of search results. Using all the tactics presented thus far won't absolutely guarantee best results, but at the very least, you will be following best practice guidelines, with the most valuable benefit of using these commands being the ability to somewhat control how your web page is described and listed in search engine results.

To check the effectiveness of the tags within your web page, there is an excellent free meta tag analyzer offered by Submit Express (www. submitexpress.com/analyzer). Use this tool to determine how you can further tweak, optimize, or revamp your site for better results. The tool allows you to see how search engine robots are analyzing your website (or competitor sites). Get tips on how to improve your meta tags, verify the keywords used, as well as check the URLs and links found on the page.

USING KEYWORDS WITHIN GRAPHICS

Another great place for keywords is in the image descriptions used to display graphics on a web page. In HTML, the **<img>** tag is used to embed, or place, an image on the page. Because spaces are not accepted within file names, hyphens are preferred. Here's an example:

<img src="graphics/volkswagen-golf-hatchback.jpg"/>

In the statement above, the "**src**" attribute stands for "source," and it supplies the name of the image while defining its location on the server relative to the current document. This image is called "volkswagen-golf-hatchback.jpg" and can be found in the "graphics" folder.

Devising and creating descriptive file names in this way provides much more information to a search engine than an image named, say, "IMG00023. jpg." Descriptively naming your images also increases the chances of them showing up for appropriate searches in engines like Google Images, giving searchers yet another way to possibly run across your magazine site.

The "**alt**" attribute can and should be used along with the "**img**" tag. The information presented in the "**alt**" tag is indexed by search engines to also help determine a page's relevance for rankings. For a user, it provides alternative information for an image in the form of words displayed in place of a graphic if that graphic cannot be displayed for some reason. Here are some of the many reasons why a graphic may not be displayed:

- A user has his or her graphics turned off.
- There is a slow connection.
- An error appears within the "**src**" attribute code.
- The user is using a text-based browser such as those found on Unix and Linux systems.
- The user uses a screen reader, which is a talking browser for the visually impaired.

With that in mind, it's a good idea to combine your keyword phrase with an accurate description of your image, which should be no longer than five words maximum. An effective use of the "**alt**" attribute may be as follows:

```
<img src="graphics/volkswagen-golf-hatchback.jpg"
            alt="Volkswagen Golf Hatchback Car"/>
```

PLACING KEYWORDS IN TEXT LINKS

When the search engines come a-searchin', they also crawl and analyze the text links found on your site, so it's of the utmost importance that these links be relevant, descriptive, and contain your keyword phrases. Because text links stand out on a page, they are actually given higher priority and more weight than any surrounding text. Knowing this, you should never have worthless links that simply read "Click Here." Provide a clue as to what you're linking to with links that read "Click Here for (fill in the blank)," where the blank contains your relevant keywords.

PLACING KEYWORDS IN DOCUMENT TITLES AND URLS

When naming files, documents, and URLs, make sure to include keywords in the titles you create. Examples of good file names to use on our hypothetical golf site might include the following:

Golf-swing-tips.html
Golf-swing-instructions.html
Golf-swing-training.html
Improving-your-golf-swing-report.pdf
Improve-your-golf-instructional-video.mp4
Golf-tips-from-the-pros.mp3

KEYWORD PLACEMENT SUMMARY

Summarizing everything we have learned thus far, without overstuffing our content with keyword phrases, keywords should be placed in each of the following web page elements:

- The "title" tag
- The "description" meta tag
- H1 thru H6 header tags
- The body text or content of your document
- The file names and URLs of documents, images, and audio and video files
- The "alt" attribute used for graphic descriptions
- Link text

Tip: For "95 SEO Tips and Tricks for Powerful Search Engine Optimization," visit webdesign.about.com/od/seo/tp/seo_tips_and_tricks.01.htm. (Notice the naming convention used for this document's URL.)

Backlinks and SEO

Another factor to take into consideration when trying to up the ante in search results is the relationship you have with other websites on the Web and the number of backlinks (or inbound links) you receive from them. Search engines presume that if you have a lot of sites linking to you, then you must be providing valuable, resourceful information. In particular, Google's PageRank is one of the methods used to calculate the relevance and importance of a web page. Its algorithm interprets a link from page A to page B as a vote by page A for page B. It measures both the quantity *and* quality (whether they come from reputable, important, high-ranking sites) of incoming links.

Don't be tempted to participate in any of the "1,000 Backlinks for $9.99" type programs. You don't know where those links are from, what reputation the sites have, and whether any of them are blacklisted. Links from shady, questionable websites can negatively impact your rankings regardless of what other SEO techniques you employ.

In addition, search engines also check the relevancy of your inbound links. If your site's subject matter is basketball, it won't help you in the least to have a backlink from a dog grooming company's website, so stay away from backlink services where you have no control over who will be linked to you. I advise that you concentrate on creating great content, and the rest will take care of itself.

When adding outbound links from your site, make sure they highly relate to your website content and will further enhance your users' experience. To check the number of inbound and outbound links to your site, you can use Open Site Explorer (www.opensiteexplorer.org), which shows a detailed view of the page as well as the domain authority of incoming links. Use this tool to also see what sites are linking to your competitors, as these will be sites that you can possibly pitch and market your magazine to as well.

Using the Robots.txt File and "Noindex" Meta Tag

Although our aim is to create search engine-friendly pages, there may be some files or directories you do not want to show up in search results and therefore don't want to be indexed at all. A **"robots.txt"** file is a simple text file (created in any text editor such as Notepad or TextEdit) that tells search engines not to crawl or index specified files or directories on your website. This file must be placed in the root (or top level) directory of your site.

On visiting a website, the first thing a bot does is look to see whether a robots.txt file exists. If this file does not exist and is not found, then the bot assumes there are no restrictions and proceeds to crawl and index the entire site. Let's look at the format of an example file:

```
User-agent: *
Disallow: /Graphics/
Disallow: /MyDocs/exclude-this.html
```

These statements found in the robots.txt file tell all search engines (as indicated by the asterisk) not to index the Graphics directory as well as the "exclude-this.html" file found in the MyDocs directory. Note that all other files in the "MyDocs" directory will be indexed as normal. It will be necessary to create a separate "Disallow" line for every file or directory that you wish to have excluded.

Although creating a robots.txt file stops certain files and directories from being indexed from within the site itself, pages may still be indexed and appear in search results if they are linked to from other sites on the Web. The only way to completely remove a page from results (whether linked to or not) is to use the "**noindex**" meta tag, which should be added along with the other meta tags that appear within the "**head**" section of the HTML document you wish to have excluded.

<meta name="robots" content="noindex, nofollow">

This statement disallows both indexing and the following of any links contained on the page. Statements like this one may be useful if there are unfinished pages you are still working on or if there are pages you create for your own personal use that would not necessarily be of value to your visitors. For more on the robots.txt file and the "noindex" meta tag, visit The Web Robots Pages (www.robotstxt.org).

Chapter 6:
Using Social Media

Creating a Strategy

Social media has forever changed the way people connect, communicate, and discover and share information online; and it provides a free, efficient vehicle that digital publishers can use to market their titles online. With the top networks like Facebook at over a billion users, YouTube at over 800 million, and Twitter at over 500 million, that's a lot of eyeballs, and it will be your job to find your target audience of potential readers and build relationships with them by engaging them with useful, relevant, informative, and entertaining content.

To use social media effectively, it will be necessary for you to create a plan. Don't just jump out there without a clue as to your purpose or a clear understanding of what needs to be communicated, on what networks, and to whom. It's imperative that you understand your audiences' needs. A reader is always going to be asking themselves "What's in it for me?" (better known as WIIFM) so you'd better have an answer that's strong enough to make them become loyal followers, readers, and subscribers.

The first thing you'll want to do is define your goals for using social media as a marketing tool. What is it exactly that you want to accomplish?

Do you want to raise awareness of your magazine, establish yourself (or your magazine) as an expert or authority in the field, increase website traffic, build loyalty, develop a community, acquire a load of fans and followers, or boost subscription sales, etc.? Having a set of objectives will help you prioritize and determine the necessary steps you need to take to accomplish your goals. These objectives also provide relevant indicators that can help you measure just how well you're doing.

Next, you will need to find out what's important to your readers. From the research you have done thus far, especially after having undertaken your keyword research strategies, you already have a good idea of what subjects and topics your audience is interested in talking about. Don't forget to use social networks to poll your audience to receive firsthand knowledge on the subjects they'd like to read or discuss and also use the networks to get feedback from your audience so that you can gauge your performance and find out what you need to do to improve efforts and keep them satisfied.

Know that true (and real) communication consists of 50 percent listening and 50 percent talking. Listening is going to be the single most important skill for you to practice when using social media effectively, and it should be carried out on a continuous basis so that you can find out and keep up with exactly what's important to your readers and create engaging two-way (I repeat, two-way) conversations from there. The rule is (just as your mother taught you) listen first, then talk. (See "Using Social Media Listening Tools" in Chapter 4.)

After you've defined your goals and researched your audience and your competition, it's time to decide what type of content and information you plan to share. What do you think your audience will find most valuable? To develop engaging, relevant content, think of things that people want, or things that motivate them. Examples include the following:

- To be liked and appreciated
- To find love and commitment
- To build a strong self-image

- To achieve better health and longer lives
- To lead more fulfilling lives
- To be more attractive to the opposite sex
- To attain financial security and wealth
- To be entertained and have fun
- To find solutions to their problems
- To know how to save time and be more efficient
- To gain knowledge or expertise on a particular subject
- To learn how to perform a task
- To receive buying advice on products and services
- To be self-sufficient, including owning their own business
- To understand their place in the overall scheme of things
- To gain clarity and direction
- To be motivated and inspired
- To find inner peace
- To be successful
- To express themselves by sharing personal stories and experiences

Also, think about how often you plan on communicating with your audience and what networks you intend to use. Where do you think you can most likely and easily connect with the potential readers of your magazine? What networks will be most appropriate for your content? For example, Twitter is great for short bursts of information (tweets are 140 characters or less) or for publishing links and teasers to articles, while Facebook is ideal for telling stories and having real conversations with your audience. YouTube is wonderful for showcasing video, and Pinterest and Instagram are great for telling stories visually. A 2012 study by ROI Research found that 44 percent of respondents are more likely to engage with a brand if the company posts pictures than any other media, so keep that in mind as you make decisions on what networks you will use.

As you create your accounts across the networks, remember to include your most important keywords within your magazine profile's bio or description. Make the information presented there both interesting and descriptive, as well as searchable. Be sure to include a link that points readers to the most important page of your website. Brand pages on sites like Facebook, Twitter, Google+, and Instagram by prominently displaying your magazine's logo and including a compelling cover image.

When posting information, never aim to overtly (and annoyingly) sell you magazine. Social networks are primarily about being social and providing value, so encourage conversation by regularly posting interesting and relevant content. Good content allows for interaction and dialogue, and it should spark conversation not only directly with you (the magazine) but between the members of your audience as well.

Spice up your posts with real-time news updates, links to articles, links to content from other providers (become a resource), sneak previews, interesting photos and videos, behind-the-scenes stories and footage, inspirational quotes, games, polls, quizzes, coupons, occasional contests, and special offers that are exclusive to your subscribers. Always use language that is both natural (no jargon allowed) and conversational. Be an active participant and regularly respond to comments to keep the conversation going. Don't let any of your accounts resemble a ghost town. If you're not regularly hanging out and having fun, then your readers won't either.

As your magazine gets underway and you begin to work out the kinks that will inevitably be involved in the creation process, I recommend that you start out using no more than two to three social networks and graduate from there. Don't give up too soon, however. Social strategies are not short-term strategies, and just like offline relationships, building lasting relationships with your audience online will take time. Be both patient and consistent. As long as you stay dedicated, relevant, and authentic, your efforts should pay off over time.

Regularly review Google Analytics (but not obsessively) to see which networks are sending the most traffic to your website or use the analytic tools supplied by the social networking sites themselves to see what types of content or communications garnered the most response. Refine (or adjust) your social media strategy according to the results that you find and the insights that you gain.

Magazines to Observe

The following sections present a diverse set of print and digital magazine brands that are faring exceptionally well across the networks. They have large, extremely engaged followers, and there's a lot to be learned from them. Closely study each one; check their strategies to see how you can best leverage the social networks that you plan to use.

FACEBOOK

Facebook (www.facebook.com) is the number one social network and the second most visited site on the Net, runner-up to none other than Google. An unparalleled distribution channel with over one billion pieces of content shared every day, Facebook offers you one of the most powerful tools you can use to connect, engage, and build relationships with your audience online. Set up a Facebook Page (you'll find the "Magazine" option listed under the Entertainment category), which is public, viewable to all (whether registered on Facebook or not), and allows anyone to become a "fan" and receive the updates you post by simply "Liking" your Page. Make sure to add Facebook "Like" buttons to your website and any articles (or content) that you publish online.

Tip: With Facebook Pages, you can customize your URL with your magazine's name so that your address will read www.facebook.com/yourmagname. The only requirement is that you have more than twenty-five fans. To register your customized URL, go to: www.facebook.com/username.

Magazine Name	Facebook ID	No. of Likes
Cosmopolitan Magazine	Cosmopolitan	2,207,607
The Economist	TheEconomist	1,433,700
Newsweek	Newsweek	250,936
Reader's Digest	Readers Digest	1,204,995
Seventeen Magazine	seventeenmagazine	1,851,044

TWITTER

Twitter (www.twitter.com) is a real-time microblogging platform where you broadcast short messages (called tweets) that consist of up to 140 characters in length. The network is based on the premise that you use your outgoing messages to answer the question of "What's happening?" But those 140 characters can be used for so much more. You can "retweet" (or repost) and share the content of others, receive private Direct Messages (DMs) from users who are following you and you are following back (that's the criteria), and use the @ sign to publicly start a conversation with, or reply to absolutely anybody who exists in Twitterland. For instance, I could send a tweet that reads "@magazinexyz enjoyed the article on The Top Ten Beauty Mistakes People Make that was published today, thanks," and you could reply with the following tweet: "@lorraine_ phill glad you enjoyed it, look out for more next month." The hashtag (#) symbol allows you to categorize your tweets by keyword in a way that makes them searchable and findable on Twitter. For instance, if your area of expertise is social media marketing, you may want to end your tweets that are relevant to the subject with "#smm" so that people interested in the topic can easily find and follow you. On the other hand, you can use the hashtag symbol to perform a real-time search to find people who are currently having conversations or asking questions about your particular subject matter. This allows you to immediately connect with them and start a conversation right away. Visit Tagdef (www.tagdef.com) for a hashtag directory. If using this network for your magazine, be sure to add Twitter "Follow" and "Tweet" buttons to your website and articles.

Magazine Name	Twitter ID	No. of Followers
Entertainment Weekly	@EW	2,497,854
InStyle	@InStyle	2,350,156
People Magazine	@PeopleMag	4,693,960
Time	@Time	4,398,751
wired	@wired	1,882,513

PINTEREST

Pinterest (www.pinterest.com) is a visual bookmarking site that allows you to "pin" images and videos to virtual pinboards that you categorize according to a subject or theme. Users have the ability to like, comment on, or have a conversation about a pin. People can follow you or your pinboards. They can "repin" your content onto their own boards, and you can in turn follow users or their boards and can repin their content onto your own boards. It is possible to create group boards that allow you to collaborate with others you decide to invite as contributors. According to social media analytics firm ZoomSphere, magazines are top performers on Pinterest, accounting for more than fifteen of the fifty most followed commercial entities currently appearing on the network. If using Pinterest as part of your social media strategy, make sure to add a "Pin It" button to photos and videos that appear on your website or in articles to encourage readers to pin and share your information to their boards. Because each pin added using the "Pin It" button links back to the website it was sourced from, Pinterest is known to be a wonderful traffic generator. The only social networking site that currently drives more traffic than Pinterest is Facebook.

Magazine Name	Pinterest ID	No. of Pins	No. of Followers
Better Homes and Gardens	bhg	4,924	331,239
Elle	elle	4,594	105,603
Martha Stewart Living	ms_living	6,778	299,117
Real Simple	realsimple	5,185	278,085
Women's Health Magazine	womenshealthmag	1,544	185,558

INSTAGRAM

Instagram (www.instagram.com) is a social network and mobile app that allows users to take pictures and share them either on Instagram itself or on other popular networks such as Facebook and Twitter. When you launch the Instagram app from a mobile device it effectively takes the place of the default camera app and provides a bunch of fun filters that allow you to creatively change the appearance of a snap. According to Digital Buzz (www.digitalbuzzblog.com), over one billion photos have been taken with the app, fifty-eight photos are uploaded every second, and about eighty-one comments are posted each second. Just like Twitter, you can use hashtags to categorize your magazine's content. For more options than are offered through the Instagram interface, you can use tools such as Statigram (statigr.am) to better manage your community, administer photo contests, and track the performance of your magazine through the use of analytic tools.

Magazine Name	Instagram ID	No. of Photos	No. of Followers
GQ	gq	1,263	315,227
Interview Magazine	interviewmag	573	58,190
Nylon Magazine	nylonmag	1,584	285,348
Rolling Stone	rollingstone	347	261,708
Teen Vogue	teenvogue	1,309	391,703

GOOGLE+

Google+ (plus.google.com) presents another platform on which you can engage and interact with your audience online. Just like the other networks, you can post content updates of various kinds, and people who have selected to follow you will see them appear in their stream. They can either comment on, share, or "+1" a post (which is the equivalent of a Facebook "Like" and ultimately gives a stamp of approval). When you post content to Google+ (hashtags can also used on the network), it is immediately indexed by Google's search engine, which allows for greater exposure. Also, Google's personalized search function means that when you post content to Google+, that content is more likely to appear in your followers' search results for relevant searches that take place on Google's website. Google Hangouts allow magazines to reach out and connect with their audience through live, face-to-face video chats, and Google Communities allow you to further connect with and gain insight from readers by creating, joining, or participating in groups with those who share similar interests. If you are planning to use this network, make sure to add Google +1 buttons to both your website and magazine articles.

Magazine Name	Google+ ID	No. of Followers
Forbes	+Forbes	730,483
Glamour	+glamour	1,387,425
Martha Stewart	+MarthaStewart	1,902,760
The New Yorker	+newyorker	160,947
Sports Illustrated	+sportsillustrated	876,956

Tip: As you use the networks and start to share links, whether it's to your own content or the content of others, the services provided by Google URL Shortener (goo.gl) and bitly (bit.ly) allow you to shorten lengthy URLs, making it much easier for you to share, tweet, or email them. Both services provide click statistics that allow you to measure the number of clicks your links receive.

Chapter 7:
Creating Your Magazine's Website

Why You Should Hire a Designer

A website may be used if you do not plan on providing regular content updates and if the pages presented are to remain more or less static, not requiring much input or conversation from your audience which can now be accomplished through social media. A website–in the traditional meaning–somewhat functions like an online brochure and can be used by a publisher to display magazine editions or downloads, collect subscription purchases, link to social media accounts, build email lists, give background information on the magazine or its contributors, and provide contact details (ad sales, submissions, support, general inquiries, etc.).

Setting up a website will be much more expensive and a lot more involved than setting up a blog. (Know that it is possible to set up a blog in a way that makes it look, display, and function like a static website, or you may decide to set up a website that includes a blog.) Unless you are truly familiar with web design principles, a master at computer languages (e.g., HTML, CSS, Perl, Ajax, and PHP), and a skilled graphic designer, then I do not recommend that you attempt to build the site yourself.

Web design covers many disciplines—which evolve daily—and it will take a considerable amount of time to learn each one as well as learn how to integrate them all successfully. Forget picking up any of those HTML for Dummies-type books. You should be fully emerged in the process of putting your magazine together, so I highly suggest that you hire a professional for the job.

Professional web designers specialize in presenting information (or content) in a way that is functional, efficient, and aesthetically pleasing. Your site must be built around audience needs, so make sure it is easy for readers to navigate and find information quickly. We've all visited those hideous, frustrating sites—never to return again, which is exactly what we don't want to happen here. Hire a designer who has the skills, knowledge, and experience to implement the pages and features you desire. If you don't know of any professional designers personally, then check the freelance resources available online.

Hiring a professional designer can help you avoid the following web faux pas:

- Nonbranded, inconsistent, incohesive design
- Slow-loading pages and graphics
- Unclear navigation where users cannot easily recognize what page they are on or identify where they need to go
- Nondescriptive navigation that does not clearly communicate the information contained on each page
- Frustrating menus that function incorrectly
- A website that is not targeted toward a particular audience (e.g., a site aimed at teens should look different from a site aimed at retirees)
- Important pages (such as the subscriptions page) buried too deep within the site, making it difficult for readers to find relevant information quickly
- Browser incompatibility, where your site displays and acts differently depending on which browser, browser version, platform, or device it is being viewed on

- The use of fonts that are not available on all computers, resulting in the site looking different depending on which platform or device it is being viewed on
- A design that is not optimized for mobile devices
- Not using effective SEO techniques
- Not including social media sharing functions
- The use of Flash, which is quickly becoming a legacy technology and is not supported by iOS devices such as the iPad and iPhone
- Lack of contrast or use of an unpleasant color scheme
- A cluttered design
- Overuse of annoying, blinking, or flashing banner ads or graphics
- Hard-to-read text due to choice of background color, text size, or text color
- Orphan pages that do not provide a way back to the originating page, forcing users to click the browser's "Back" button
- Broken links that either do nothing or lead nowhere, resulting in the "Page Cannot Be Found" error message
- Vertical scrolling (Just say NO!)

Questions to Ask Your Designer or Web Design Firm

If you decide to hire a web designer, you will need to ask the following questions:

Is there an online portfolio I can view?

Most designers showcase completed projects online. Check to make sure their work exemplifies the style, flair, and design characteristics you are looking for. It will be great if they have had experience developing other online magazines. Make sure to use my web faux pas checklist to evaluate their level of competency.

Will you be working from a template, or will you create an original design?

Because of your specific needs, a designer will probably suggest that you go with an original design. A template-based site, however, can be customized according to your particular requirements. Request quotes for both and ask to view example template designs. If developing a WordPress site, then it will be easy enough for you to hunt down a theme that you can have customized for your needs.

Will pages be optimized for search engines?

Armed with the information presented in Chapter 5, it is important that your designer understands how to structure pages in a way that works best for SEO.

Will the site be mobile friendly?

Your website should be optimized for mobile reading so that it can easily be viewed on smaller screens and devices. Mobile-friendly sites include features such as large buttons; simple, thumb-friendly navigation; easy-to-access search functions; and a limited amount of pinching, scrolling, and zooming needed in order to view content. Ask for examples of the designer's most recently designed mobile-friendly websites and view them on a variety of devices (including your desktop or laptop) to ensure that all formats allow for a positive user experience.

Is it possible for you to implement newsletter sign-up, survey, or contact form scripts?

Scripts should be set up to send all information directly to your email address. Have your designer create an autoresponder that automatically sends a confirmation email to the recipient's address. If it's an inquiry from your contact form, don't take long to respond. Having a reasonably fast response rate is an important feature of your site, as it lets visitors know you are there and that you care.

Can you set up a "members-only" section of the website that is accessed through sign-up or a paid subscription?

There are various options and scripts availablle online that will allow for members-only access to predefined content on your site. Ensure that your designer is familiar with the process and is able to implement this solution if required. Provide your designer with a list of the type of information you need to capture from the subscriptions page for your database, such as name, address, phone number, email address, date of subscription, subscription length, amount paid, etc.

Can you make it easy for users to share information with their social media networks?

Expand your audience by ensuring that social media sharing buttons are set up on your site. Have your designer suggest viable options for doing this or simply discuss the sites AddThis (www.addthis.com) and ShareThis (www.sharethis.com) with him or her.

Will I be able to handle site updates myself?

The answer to this question will vary according to what solution your designer decides to implement for you and what web skills you possess. If this option is important to you, then say so at the onset of the project to make the designer aware of your needs. With content management systems (such as WordPress and Drupal) that allow for easy updating by non–tech savvy users, this should not be a problem, but updating a website will be much more labor intensive and will require you to know a little HTML and possibly CSS too.

If you are not using a content management system and you are not particularly tech savvy, then you are advised to check into a product offered by Adobe called Contribute (available for both Mac and PC). Contribute allows nontechnical folks to quickly and easily edit website content directly from their browser window. Its interface and functionality are very similar to those of Microsoft Word, so if you can use Word, then you can use Contribute too.

What information will I need to provide to generate an estimate for the entire project?

Please see the next section of this chapter entitled "Information You May Need to Provide." Know that you are responsible for the accuracy of the information supplied; it is not your designer's job to correct spelling or fix bad grammar.

What will be the approximate cost?

Submit requests to at least three designers for price comparison. Even better, if you use an online freelance provider service, designers will bid at competitive rates for your project.

What are the payment terms?

All design shops function differently, but you will receive a proposal or estimate that is usually valid for thirty days, based on the project specifications and the anticipated scope of the work. When you approve and sign off on the estimate, you will usually need to deposit at least 50 percent of the total amount, with the balance due upon prototype sign-off as discussed below.

How long will it take to complete the design?

This will depend on the complexity of the project and your designer's anticipated workload at the time.

What is the usual development process? What checkpoints and milestones will there be along the way?

After you sign off on the estimate, pay the deposit, and supply your designer with all the information needed, he or she will create either a prototype web page, a sketch, or a printout that demonstrates the general page layout of your site. In the case of a prototype, actual functionality will not be implemented until later on in the process. The sample layout will demonstrate the colors, fonts, navigation, buttons, logo and graphics placement, and any other design-related elements that are pertinent to the project.

What happens if I do not like the design?

If, as you work with your designer to refine the design, you just can't seem to see eye to eye and he or she seems incapable of implementing your ideas, then it will be necessary for you to cut ties and pay the money owed thus far. If you take time to find a designer who comes with a recommendation, matches your style, and has produced work you are impressed with, then this scenario should not arise.

What happens if I decide to cancel the project?

This will depend on how far along in the process you are when you decide to cancel the project. Charges for services rendered may be 25 percent to 50 percent if the work is canceled during the initial design phase, 50 percent if canceled after the completion and sign-off on the prototype, and 100 percent if canceled after the final design is complete.

How are revisions and alterations handled along the way?

If the revisions or alterations are deemed within scope, as according to the original proposal, then they are already included as part of the estimated fee. If developments require new items or functionality that are deemed out of scope or were not defined within the original estimate, then a new proposal and estimate will have to be generated.

How is website compatibility testing handled? What browsers and platforms do you test on?

Your website should be tested to ensure it acts and looks the same regardless of platform, operating system, browser, or device used. At a minimum, insist that your site be tested on both Mac and PC and a couple different mobile devices as well as in various browsers, including Firefox, Internet Explorer, Google Chrome, and Safari.

Will you provide tech support? If so, for how long?

Most designers will offer free technical support for anywhere from seven to thirty days after your site goes live, providing an opportunity to work out any minor quirks, bugs, or tweaks you discover. Use this period to thoroughly go through your site to ensure that it functions and displays exactly as required.

Information You May Need to Provide

Here is some information you may need to provide to your designer to receive an accurate estimate and timeline for your website design:

- What is your magazine's name?
- What is the tag line or slogan?
- What is your editorial philosophy? Why do you exist?
- Who is your target audience?
- What are the goals and objectives of your site?
- What is the desired theme, style, or appearance of your site? For example, are you hip, funky, professional, feminine, conservative, trustworthy? Find a few adjectives that describe your style.
- Give your designer an idea of how you would like your site to appear by providing the URLs of three websites that you like and three that you do not. Tell him what you do and don't like about each one.
- What are your preferred colors? Supply color samples for accuracy.
- Are there any colors you absolutely dislike?
- How many subject categories will your website have?
- What are the names and descriptions of the pages that will appear in each category?
- Will you include any special site features or functionality such as RSS feeds, social media sharing capabilities, a newsletter sign-up form, a subscription sales area, members-only access pages, quizzes, polls, flip books, or downloadable files?
- What materials do you plan to provide (e.g., logo, copy, images, video, podcasts)?
- What is your desired date of completion?

Chapter 8:
Creating Your Magazine's Blog

WordPress CMS

A content management system (CMS) is a software tool that allows for the creation, editing, publishing, distribution, and discovery of electronic content such as text, images, graphics, video, sound, and documents. A blog constitutes a CMS, and it enables a user to freely and easily publish to the Web, through a Web-based interface, with no official technical knowledge or training necessary. This is the primary reason why blogs are so popular and in such widespread use today.

A magazine's blog will differ from that of a traditional blog. A blog is typically defined as being the personal platform of a single author who has a particular interest or point of view on a specified subject, and is written in a conversational tone. A magazine blog will differ in its approach to content creation and delivery in that there will be several contributors who publish according to a set schedule, providing varied content that is centered around a basic theme (divided into departments, columns, and features). The most distinguishing fact between the two is that quality control (which can include fact-checking, researching, and correcting errors in grammar, syntax, punctuation, and spelling) is performed on all content by an editorial staff.

Several content management systems, such as Drupal and Joomla, are available but with over 60 million installations of the software worldwide, WordPress is rated as the number one content management system on the Web today. The software is freely available for download, and if you already have a domain name and web host (as the software requires installation on a web server), it can easily be installed to your website through the control panel. Check with your host for details; it is literally a one-click set-up process.

WordPress's number one rating is due in large part to the unlimited number of add-ons, plug-ins, themes, tools, and features available, giving you the flexibility to both create and grow your magazine's blog any which way you may need to in the future. Depending on your specifications and feature requirements, you may need to hire a developer or designer who can brand your site with an appropriately tweaked theme (or create one from scratch) as well as install the various plug-ins and widgets you may require. However, numerous tutorials and step-by-step guides are available online that can show you how to carry out most of these functions yourself.

Tip: For a list of "Essential WordPress Plug-ins," please see Appendix A.

Selecting a WordPress Theme

A WordPress theme, or template, will allow you to create the design, look, feel, and structure of your magazine's blog. There are literally thousands of themes available online, and the process of selecting one can be both time consuming and overwhelming. The following criteria should help make the process of selecting a theme a little easier for you.

1. Ensure the template you select works with the latest version of WordPress. Visit www.wordpress.org for information on the most current release.
2. If possible, steer away from free WordPress themes as they often contain encrypted code in the footer section of the template that is protected from editing and can stop a site from working altogether if tampered with. If a free theme is downloaded from an obscure website, then there is also the risk of it containing malicious code that can end up being disastrous for a site.
3. Choose a theme that is flexible and has the most customization options. Keep in mind that you will probably want to tweak your magazine's blog by either adding more functionality or changing its structure later on down the line.
4. Confirm that the theme is SEO friendly, has plenty of SEO features, and will work with major plug-ins (such as WordPress SEO by Yoast) to ensure your site's visibility on the Web.
5. Ensure the template is "widget ready." Most widgets enable a user to customize theme sidebars according to layout needs by adding functionality, such as listing the most recent posts, the most popular posts, or displaying relevant ads.
6. Make sure the theme includes social media integration with "Share" buttons that show alongside content. Other considerations may be "Follow" or "Like" buttons and the ability to display your Twitter or Facebook stream.
7. If the option exists, go for a responsive, fluid, adaptive WordPress theme that automatically adjusts to a visitor's screen size and allows your website to display perfectly on any device whether desktop, tablet, e-reader, or smartphone.
8. Check the license to find out whether you receive free support, if you are entitled to unlimited updates at no extra cost, whether there's a money-back guarantee, and if there are any restrictions associated with the use of the template.

POPULAR THEME PROVIDERS

There are numerous reputable websites where you can purchase and download themes online. The following six are among the most popular providers. And just so you know, a high percentage of the most well-known and respected bloggers on the Net either use StudioPress or Thesis.

Elegant Themes (www.elegantthemes.com)
Press75 (www.press75.com)
Solostream (www.solostream.com/wordpress-themes)
StudioPress (www.studiopress.com)
Thesis (www.diythemes.com)
WooThemes (www.woothemes.com)

Blogging and SEO

It's a well known fact that search engines just love blogs. Topic-specific, regularly updated blogs are rewarded by Google and other search engines with higher page rankings. As Rick Bruner, former research director of DoubleClick, put it, "Blog stands for Better Listings On Google." Frequently updated content means that spiders return regularly to re-index your content and ensure they always have the latest, most current information from your site.

"The squeaky wheel gets the grease," as they say, so people searching for information on your particular subject matter will find you more quickly through a regularly updated blog than they would through a static website that does not have a blog or is not frequently updated. Always use carefully selected keywords for your post's title, body text, tags, permalink (which is the URL that points to a specific blog post after it has passed from the front page into the archives), as well as the names of any graphics, audio and video files, or link text you incorporate.

Another advantage a blog has over a static website is the ability to receive "trackbacks." A trackback is an automated alert that is sent to a blog owner to let him or her know that a particular post has been linked to or referenced from another site. Most blogging software supports trackbacks. According to the settings of the particular platform, a trackback sends the name of the site that's referencing it, the URL, the title of the post, and a short excerpt of the contents. What's really great about this is that a trackback will automatically create a comment on the original post that was referenced; this comment provides a link to the new post, giving readers the opportunity to discover blogs within the same subject category, which can result in an increased amount of incoming traffic for the blogger who made the reference. Linking to, or referencing, posts from other blog sites that appear within your niche can be used as a technique to get your publication noticed. It can also serve as a method for creating an abundance of inbound links. But don't abuse this trackback functionality. Make sure your readers are truly benefiting from the information that you link to and share.

> **Tip:** For an easy way to generate links and get help with SEO, link the main keywords in your blog post to other relevant documents on your site at least once within the body text. Although internal linking is not as important as links from external sites, it still helps. When linking this way, make sure to use the full URL, including the "http://" part of the address.

Ideas for Blog Promotion

Here are a few ideas you can use to promote your magazine blog:

- Ensure all blog posts are SEO friendly.
- Submit new posts to search engines and directories. (See "Ping Your Website or Blog" in Chapter 4.)
- Include social media sharing buttons for networks such as Facebook, Twitter, Pinterest, and Google+ to make it easy for readers to share content with their networks.

- Incorporate both RSS and email subscription capability. (See "Understanding RSS" in Chapter 4.)
- Announce your best and most relevant posts via email and on Facebook, Twitter, or other social networking sites. If posting to Twitter, use the hashtag symbol as it relates to your subject matter (e.g., #beautytips).
- Bookmark and tag your best articles on sites like Digg (www.digg.com), Delicious (www.delicious.com), reddit (www.reddit.com), and StumbleUpon (www.stumbleupon.com).
- Search for questions on Twitter and LinkedIn that relate to your particular subject and respond by presenting links to meaningful blog posts or articles on your magazine's site.
- Participate in other communities. Visit related forums, groups, and blogs to leave feedback or answer questions, linking to posts or articles from your site that relate to the question at hand.
- Network and build relationships with popular bloggers and magazines in your field who already have established audiences. After a relationship is established, ask for links to your content.
- Widen your audience by having some of your writers guest post on other blogs or magazine sites. Always include a link back to your magazine's blog in the byline.
- Use Google Analytics to find out which sites are sending you the most traffic and consider building relationships with them.
- Find out who is linking to the popular blogs in your subject category by going to Google and typing in "link:www.the-blogs-name.com." Use the list to generate inbound links by promoting your magazine's content to these sites using the methods discussed thus far.
- Claim your blog at Technorati.com so that you will be added to Technorati's Blog Directory for the categories you specify. Claiming your blog at the site will also allow you to see who's linking to you from other sites in their directory. This presents another great way for you to start and build valuable relationships online.

- Add your blog's URL to your email signature, business cards, website (if separate), press kit, press releases, brochures, flyers, and any other promotional materials you may have.

Note: I do not advise syndicating your blog content across all social networks and announcing every single post or article you create, as people who follow you across several networks may view this behavior as somewhat "spammy." Instead, I suggest you only post your best, most relevant, and most valuable content to other networks.

Measuring Your Blog's Success

Everybody will have different criteria, according to their desired goals, for measuring a blog's success. Potential advertisers will also be interested to know the following information, so make sure to include it as part of your media kit after your traffic picks up. A blog's success can be measured by any of the following:

- The number of visits
- The number of visitors
- The number of new visitors versus the number of returning visitors
- The number of page views per visit
- How long visitors stay engaged on the site
- The number of comments received
- The quality of comments received
- The general feedback received
- How many people are citing and linking to your blog
- The number of "shares" you receive to social networks
- The number of RSS subscriptions
- The number of newsletter sign-ups
- Search engine rankings

- The number of magazine subscriptions that came as a result of your blogging activities. (Note that if you are performing numerous online marketing activities, then the results from one particular effort can be hard to determine or track without the use of a specific URL or purchase code.)

Chapter 9:
Digital Magazine Design

General Guidelines

Much like your magazine's name, your logo stands for everything your magazine represents and is the cornerstone of your brand. It should be attention getting, legible, distinctive, and memorable. It's the first thing your reader sees that ultimately conveys a message, mood, and feeling about your magazine. Make sure it looks professional and stands out enough to differentiate you from your competitors.

Your logo should have the ability to be incorporated into everything from business cards to promotional materials, and it should be made from a custom-designed font that cannot easily be replicated. It can be designed using type only, which is called a logotype, or it can be a combination of a symbol and typography.

Your cover is the most important page of your magazine, so it must immediately grab attention and successfully communicate your entire magazine's message or theme. Create catchy, intriguing, benefit-oriented cover lines that entice readers to open it up. All available elements—the logo, image, copy, color, composition, and type—must effectively work together to quickly and clearly communicate what your magazine is all about. Using a photograph on the cover is preferred to an illustration. Try not to use stock photography on the cover, as the image may have already been seen elsewhere. Aim for an original image and spare no expense in its creation. Also, don't forget, this is digital . . . so think of innovative ways you can use video or other interactive elements as part of your cover design as well. For an example of a dynamic, digital cover, see the Digital Magazine Awards' 2012 Magazine Cover of the Year at www. digitalmagazineawards.com.

> **Note:** You can find winners and finalists of this year's Best Magazine Cover Contest as awarded by the American Society of Magazine Editors (ASME) at www.magazine.org/asme.

During the design process, you will have to decide what fonts you will use throughout your magazine. Although your computer comes with hundreds of pre-installed fonts, you only need two: one for the headlines and one for the body text. Two fonts are sufficient, as a font family may contain numerous styles (italic, bold, extra bold, condensed, etc.) that affect the look, shape, and weight of the letters. This allows enough room to provide for both consistency and variety. Although you may deviate and use a special font for impact as a story demands, the general consensus is that the use of too many fonts does not allow for a cohesive design and can be visually confusing to a reader.

The two basic classifications of font faces are serif and sans serif. Serif fonts have curlicues at the ends of the letters, and sans serif fonts do not. Research shows that serif fonts are easier to read, as the serifs of the letters serve as a guideline for the eye. With that in mind, choose a serif font for your body text, which should ALWAYS be the same leading and point size throughout the publication. Use a sans serif font for your headlines, subheads, and sidebars. Examples of serif fonts include Times New Roman, Baskerville, Garamond, Bodoni, and Palatino. Examples of sans serif fonts include Arial, Helvetica, Futura, Avante Garde, and Myriad.

The graphics that appear within your magazine should be carefully selected to clearly illustrate and convey the right feeling about a story. You should not have to actually read a headline or subtitle to get the gist of a story. Videos should be short, engaging, and to the point; they must be helpful and relevant to your reader. Use them as appropriate to further enhance your content offerings.

Headlines should be compelling, contain keywords, and pull the reader in by arousing interest, promising a benefit, or offering helpful information. They should be short and specific and create a sense of urgency that makes the reader want to read—or at least browse—the article right away. Subtitles should elaborate on the headline; becoming the bridge between the headline and the story in a way that further captivates readers and encourages them to read on.

Your stories should be interesting, informative, unpredictable, and relevant to your audience's interests. Make sure stories are actually readable and that it is not necessary to pick up a dictionary for every other word. Talk to your readers in a voice or tone with which they are both familiar and comfortable. Make your magazine a friend, literally. Hold readers' interest with each story by taking them on a journey that has a definite beginning, middle, and end. Don't lose them halfway where they think, *What's the point? Why am I reading this story?* Use fresh ideas and try to add angles and information that have not been explored before. Lastly, your copy should be clean and not contain typos, bad grammar, misspellings, or incorrect punctuation.

Planning the Layout and Design

When deciding on how your magazine should look, the best thing to do is visit your local bookstore and browse through numerous titles that appear across different genres. Even though you will be creating a digital offering, there is still a lot to be learned from print. Identify different design elements by looking at the following attributes: What fonts and font styles are used? Are they consistent throughout the magazine? How large is the type? What about the space between the letters—are words tightly packed or loose? How about the leading (the space between the lines)? How many columns are used? How long, or short, are the line lengths? Is it easy to read—if so, why? Does the magazine appear light and airy or cramped and uncomfortable? What things make you uncomfortable? Are the left, right, and center page margins wide or narrow? How do they relate to one another? How much white space is there at the top and bottom of each article? Is this consistent throughout the magazine? Where do articles and headlines start and finish on the page? How are pictures used? Are they bled off the page? How is color used throughout the publication? Is there a specific color scheme? What elements are used to emphasize or de-emphasize sections on the page? Is the magazine graphic heavy or text heavy? Do you see a visually cohesive design throughout the publication?

Next you will need to carry out the same process, but this time studying digital magazines. In what ways do they mirror or differ from what you have already learned from their print counterparts? How are touch, tap, swipe, and scroll gestures used? How are hotspots and pop-ups used to indicate and supply extra information? Is it fun or confusing to use? What types of interactivity have been included? Are there animations, videos, slideshows, audio clips, or links to bonus materials? How is social media integrated into the publication? How easy is it for readers to share content? Is the magazine easy to navigate and jump to various sections—if so, what makes it that way? What about article lengths? Are they typically longer, shorter, or the same length as offered in print? What about the size of the publication? Is the table of contents somewhat scaled down, and are there fewer pages than would appear in a print version? What mode is the magazine presented in: landscape, portrait, or both?

As you have witnessed, print and digital are two very different mediums, and it's still very early on in the digital space, so no standard formats have been defined as of yet. As a result, there's a lot of experimentation going on. I advise you take the best of what you have learned from print and transfer these ideas over in a way that makes sense in digital, augmenting your publication with digital enhancements that cleverly move away from the restrictions of print but doing so in a way that makes it just as easy to figure out as reading a printed version. Think of how you can optimize a reader's experience on a smaller device. That could mean fewer and shorter (scannable) articles, larger text, easy navigation, bold callouts that clearly outline interactive elements, links to additional content, the use of photo galleries, the inclusion of 3-D, and so on. Aim to create an identifiable look that stands out and competes fiercely with other digital titles in the market.

Although some of you will opt to carry out the design process yourself (and most of the tools outlined in the next chapter will allow you to do so), an experienced interface designer who is familiar with designing for a digital medium can really get creative and add the bells, whistles, and fun features that can be incorporated into a digital publication. But be warned, don't overdo it; your magazine's appearance should be clean, clear, and readable with the number one goal being to inform, engage, and entertain. Never allow interface elements to overpower or distract from your content. Never overwhelm, bombard, or confuse your reader with elements that are not intuitive or that make content hard to find. Keep it simple and usable. Start out by doing just a few things exceptionally well.

Software You May Need

PAGE LAYOUT AND DESIGN SOFTWARE

In Chapter 10, we will discuss some of the options, services, and different formats you can use to get your digital magazine published. The majority of the solutions presented require that you create a PDF file that can then be embellished with digital enhancements. Page layout software is used by graphic designers to manipulate text and graphics to create documents such as newspapers, magazines, books, brochures, and posters. Here is a list of recommended layout and design software that you (or your designer) may wish to use in the design of your magazine and the creation of your PDF file.

> **Tip:** Students, instructors, and faculty staff members should check for educational licenses that allow for software from the likes of Adobe, Microsoft, and Quark to be purchased at significantly reduced prices. You can visit JourneyEd (www.journeyed.com) to learn more.

Adobe Indesign (www.adobe.com)
Description: Professional-level software regarded as the industry standard and used by graphic designers and production artists
Platform(s): Mac OS and Windows
Price: $699 (free 30-day trial available)
User level: Expert

> **Note:** With the addition of Adobe's Digital Publishing Suite (which requires a separate license and additional fees), InDesign is capable of producing fully interactive, branded digital publications for mobile devices.

Microsoft Publisher (office.microsoft.com)
Description: Intuitive presentation software that helps to deliver quality results
Platform(s): Windows
Price: $139.99
User level: Beginner

PagePlus (www.serif.com/pageplus)
Description: Desktop publishing software that comes with templates, artwork, automated assistants, and on-screen guides that help make the publishing process quick and easy
Platform(s): Windows
Price: $99.99
User level: Beginner

Pages (available from the Mac App Store)
Description: Easy-to-use page layout software that comes with over 180 document templates that are designed by Apple
Platform(s): Mac OS
Price: $19.99
User level: Beginner

PowerPoint (office.microsoft.com)
Description: Popular presentation software created by Microsoft
Platform(s): Mac OS and Windows
Price: $139.99
User level: Intermediate

QuarkXPress (www.quark.com)
Description: Professional-level software used by graphic designers and production artists. For a completely digital workflow solution, the software can be used in conjunction with App Studio as described in Chapter 10's "Customized App Solutions."
Platform(s): Mac OS and Windows
Price: $420 (free 30-day trial available)
User level: Expert

IMAGE EDITING SOFTWARE

The following tools are used for image editing and graphics creation. Some of the features and functions include resizing, cropping, color correcting, sharpening, removing objects, and applying special effects to images.

Adobe Photoshop (www.photoshop.com)
Description: Advanced image editing software considered to be the industry standard and used by professional photographers and

graphic designers
Platform(s): Mac OS and Windows
Price: $699 (free 30-day trial available)
User level: Expert

Adobe Photoshop Elements (www.photoshop.com)
Description: Known as the consumer version of Adobe Photoshop, Adobe Elements contains fewer features and simpler options but is suitable for both amateurs and professionals alike.
Platform(s): Mac OS and Windows
Price: $99.99 (free 30-day trial available)
User level: Beginner

Note: One of the key differences between Adobe Photoshop and Adobe Elements is that Elements cannot export files in the CMYK color mode without the use of a third-party plug-in. This will only be an issue if you plan on creating a print version of your magazine (ignore if only producing digital), as images must be converted to CMYK in order for your printer to be able to produce the images on paper. Some digital presses, however, are able to print RGB images (the color mode used by TV and computer monitors), so you will have to check with your particular provider to see what type of image files they require. To change or check the color mode of an image in Photoshop, go to Image > Mode.

AUDIO EDITING SOFTWARE

The following software will allow you to create, record, edit, or mix audio from a variety of sources and formats.

Adobe Audition (www.adobe.com)
Description: The software to use for professional audio production, as it offers high-performance, intuitive tools for sound recording, editing, mixing, restoration, and effects

Platform(s): Mac OS and Windows
Price: $349
User level: Expert

Audacity (audacity.sourceforge.net)
Description: Easy-to-use audio editing software that has a super user-friendly interface and is great for recording, editing, and mixing voice-overs, instructional guides, discussions, interviews, and podcasts. A bunch of effects are also included in the package.
Platform(s): Mac OS, Windows, and GNU/Linux
Price: Free (donations accepted)
User level: Beginner

GarageBand (available from the Mac App Store)
Description: A full-fledged multitrack recording studio that not only lets you record, edit, and mix sound but also includes a huge library of prerecorded instruments (pianos, organs, guitars, drums, etc.) and loops that you can use in the creation of original compositions. GarageBand comes pre-installed on all newly purchased Macs as part of the iLife suite, which also includes iPhoto, iMovie, iWeb, and iDVD.
Platform(s): Mac OS and iOS (iPad, iPhone, and iPod Touch)
Price: Mac OS $14.99; iOS $4.99
User level: Beginner

MAGIX Music Maker (www.magix.com)
Description: Multitrack music production software and audio editing tool that contains many effects and more than 3,500 sounds and loops, all accessible through a well-designed user interface
Platform(s): Windows
Price: $59.99
User level: Intermediate

VIDEO EDITING SOFTWARE

Use the following video editing software to assemble raw video footage into professional-quality video files that are ready for broadcast.

Adobe Premiere Elements (www.adobe.com)
Description: Fast and efficient video editing software that lets you choose from a storyboard or timeline view. Adobe Premiere Elements comes with the ability to combine up to ninety-nine audio and video tracks, hundreds of effects and transitions, dozens of templates, as well as high-quality audio effects and controls.
Platform(s): Mac OS and Windows
Price: $99.99 (free 30-day trial available)
User level: Intermediate

CyberLink PowerDirector (www.cyberlink.com)
Description: Considered a favorite by many, this easy-to-use home video editing software enables you to create professional-looking video projects and comes with over 300 editing tools and 100 built-in effects. There's also a huge online community where users congregate to share tips and tricks for using the software effectively.
Platform(s): Windows
Price: $79.99 (free 30-day trial with limited features available)
User level: Beginner

Final Cut Pro X (available from the Mac App Store)
Description: Professional video editing suite from Apple built to include everything needed by today's creative editors for postproduction. Suitable for creating movies, television programs, music videos, commercials, and promos, etc., its features include the ability to both import and organize media; edit audio and video; create customized

titles, transitions, and effects; color match clips; and edit multi-camera projects with automatic sync and support for up to sixty-four camera angles. Final Cut Pro breaks free from the restrictions of old-fashioned timeline tracks with the introduction of a new, dynamic editing interface that allows users to work with precision and speed.
Platform(s): Mac OS
Price: $299.99 (free 30-day trial available)
User level: Expert

iMovie (available from the Mac App Store)
Description: Built for novices but with enough power for enthusiasts, iMovie comes with a drag-and-drop interface that lets you simply drag your favorite clips into the project area. You can add stunning customized effects and arrange them in whatever sequence you'd like. Drag in titles and transitions, drop in photos, or add audio from iTunes and GarageBand. There's so much you can do. iMovie comes pre-installed on all newly purchased Macs as part of the iLife suite, which also includes GarageBand, iPhoto, iWeb, and iDVD.
Platform(s): Mac OS and iOS (iPad, iPhone, and iPod Touch)
Price: Mac OS $14.99; iOS $4.99
User level: Beginner

MAGIX Movie Edit Pro (www.magix.com)
Description: User-friendly, versatile video editor that gives you the option of manually or automatically editing sound and video; includes 3-D support; and offers an extensive selection of professional video and audio effects, transitions, animated menu templates, thematic intros and outros, and decorative features
Platform(s): Windows
Price: $99.99
User level: Beginner

Who's Doing It Well

The Digital Magazine Awards (DMA) is an international awards celebrating the best magazines, individuals, and advertisers from the digital publishing industry. Chairman Bruce Hudson initiated the awards as a form of inspiration and a way to keep track of how digital magazines are evolving. In 2012, *Post Magazine* won for Overall Magazine of the Year. The judges described *Post* as "a new concept executed to near perfection. This is a phenomenally beautiful magazine, wonderfully designed and conceptualized. It takes the idea of structure in digital content and plugs it into the mains. This magazine ushers in a new era of digital magazines." For a list of DMA 2012 winners, visit www.digitalmagazineawards.com.

iMonitor is an extensive database that tracks U.S. and international publications distributed through dedicated tablet apps. iMonitor currently tracks more than 3,500 apps from over 60 countries, which has allowed publishers and advertisers to share the cost of their efforts as well as provide them with the opportunity to stay abreast of developments in terms of:

- Best practices
- Evolving business models
- New apps
- Best apps
- Standout ads
- Innovative features

In November 2012, McPheters & Company (www.mcpheters.com) released a list of the Best Consumer Publication & News-Related Apps for iPad. The list is based on iMonitor's rating system, which scores each app according to the level of design, functionality, and use of rich media content. Figure 8 gives a subset of that list, showing iMonitor rankings for the best U.S.-based consumer publication apps that have been specially made for the iPad. According to CEO Rebecca McPheters, "As the number of magazine apps has exploded, the bar for outstanding performance has constantly evolved. These apps are each doing an outstanding job of fully leveraging the iPad's capabilities to enhance the user experience and expand upon the services traditionally offered to readers by printed publications."

Figure 8: iMonitor List of Best Consumer Publication Apps for iPad (USA)

App Name	Publisher	App Rating
Martha Stewart Living Magazine for iPad	Martha Stewart Living Omnimedia, Inc.	99.9%
Newsweek for iPad	Newsweek, Inc.	99.9%
Phoenix Home & Garden Magazine	Cities West Publishing, Inc.	99.9%
Reader's Digest	Reader's Digest Association	99.9%
Allure Magazine	Condé Nast	99.4%
Bloomberg Businessweek+	Bloomberg L.P.	99.4%
Condé Nast Traveler	Condé Nast	99.4%
Food & Wine Magazine	American Express Publishing Corporation	99.4%
Fortune Magazine	Time Warner	99.4%
Golf Digest Magazine	Condé Nast	99.4%
GQ	Condé Nast	99.4%
Intelligent Life	The Economist Group	99.4%
Martha Stewart Everyday Food Magazine	Martha Stewart Living Omnimedia, Inc.	99.4%
Men's Health Mag	Rodale, Inc.	99.4%
National Geographic Magazine	National Geographic Society	99.4%
Vanity Fair iPad Edition	Condé Nast	99.4%
Wired Magazine	Condé Nast	99.4%
Women's Health Mag	Rodale, Inc.	99.4%

Source: McPheters & Company iMonitor, November 2012

Chapter 10:
Creating and Proofing Your Digital Magazine

Flip Books

A flip book, or flip book-type app, can be used to provide a digital preview of your magazine on a website, blog, e-reader, or an iOS or Android device through the use of a third-party newsstand app. You can use this format to showcase entire issues (or catalogs) to subscribers, or alternatively you can provide a sample of your magazine in the form of a subset of pages so that you might encourage readers to subscribe.

Flip books can be viewed online, offline, or both. Page-turning functionality is animated to "flip" through, going backwards or forwards as you scroll, click, or drag the magazine's pages on your viewer. As well as being able to customize the look and feel of the interface, features may include print and zoom functionality, the ability to add bookmarks or notes, search capability, and the inclusion of digital properties such as video, audio, and hyperlinks that, for example, could link to back issues, more in-depth bonus information, an email address, or a social media account. Some solutions also include statistical tracking and analysis tools.

The following software solutions vary in price, feature set, and functionality. All include HTML5 and CSS support as opposed to a Flash-only solution, which cannot be viewed on an iOS device. Your goal should always be to create documents that can be viewed anywhere, anytime, and on any device. I personally evaluated and tested numerous flip book-type applications, and I found the following three to be the most flexible, user friendly, intuitive to use, and current in features.

FLIP BOOK SOFTWARE

3D Issue (www.3dissue.com)
3D issue is available for both Mac and PC. It allows you to create digital magazines for online and offline viewing on desktops, laptops, iPads, iPhones, Android devices, tablets, and e-readers such as Kindle, Nook, Sony, and others. By far one of the more robust offerings for this type of software, the Pro version includes an impressive array of features: a lifetime license available for one installation or domain, both HTML5 and Flash file outputs, customization options, page-flip and pinch-zoom animations, PDF download and printing ability, keyword and phrase search capability, bookmarks and notes features, search engine compatibility, automatic link detection, rich media elements (links, videos, audio), social media sharing functions, Google Analytics integration, the ability to archive previous issues, ad banner advertising, and .EPUB and .MOBI e-reader outputs. It also offers apps specifically made for the iPad, iPhone, Android, Facebook, and a desktop offline reader. Note that the iOS and Android versions of your magazine have to be viewed on 3D Issue's proprietary Digital Magazine App, which is available for free from Apple's App Store and Google Play, respectively. Pricing starts at $499 for the lite version, with the Pro costing $1,299; a 30-day free trial is also available.

eMagStudio (www.emagcreator.com)
Available for both Mac and PC, eMagStudio is a fully customizable publishing solution that allows you to create a branded, interactive magazine for both online and offline viewing. PDF files are used to create browser-based Flash- and HTML5-compatible versions of your publication that can be viewed on mobile and tablet platforms such as the iPad, iPhone, and Android devices. eMagApp is a free application available from Apple's App Store and Google Play, and it will be necessary for iOS and Android devices to view the magazines that are created with the software (if not viewing through a browser window). Here are some of its key features: page-flip and zoom animations; PDF download and printing ability; keyword and phrase search capability; a bookmarks feature; and the ability to add interactive content such as video (which can be streamed directly from YouTube), audio, hyperlinks, flash animations, and slideshows that can be used to display rotating banner ads or image galleries. It is possible to stream RSS feeds directly to your magazine, and social media sharing functions are included. eMagStudio also offers a hosting service for those who require it, and the software boasts a reader tracking and statistics module that can be used to provide detailed insight into reader behavior. Yearly licenses start from $139 a month, with a lifetime license priced at $2,499. New customers are offered free, customized, start-up training, and a limited trial version is available online.

FlippingBook Publisher (www.flippingbook.com)
FlippingBook Publisher is a Windows-based software application that allows you to import PDF, Word, PowerPoint, and other file types for the creation of a standalone digital magazine. Publications support both Flash and HTML5 standards, so they can be viewed on any device that has access to a web browser. The software also has the capability to create files for offline distribution (CD, DVD, or flash drive), creating an .EXE file for PCs and an .APP file for Macs.

It includes the following functions: page-flip and zoom animations, PDF download and printing ability, text search capability, search engine optimization, video integration, Facebook and Twitter social media sharing functions, Google Analytics support, and a quick preview function that allows you to test and see how your publication will look on different devices such as the iPad, iPhone, and Android mobile phones. The basic version starts at $299, with the professional version priced at $399; a limited trial version is available online.

Integrative Online Solutions for Digital Publishers

Another alternative for publishing a digital magazine comes in the form of an online newsstand service that allows you to create digital interactive content that can be hosted on either the service provider's website or your own. With these types of solutions, you don't have to actually create a website or blog to showcase your publication, as they provide a one-stop shop for all you need to do to get your publication online. Large publishers like Hearst, Time Warner, and Condé Nast tend to use the services provided by companies such as Zinio (www.zinio.com) and Next Issue (www.nextissue.com) among others; the following newsstand services, however, may be better suited for small to mid-size, budget-conscious, start-up publishers.

NEWSSTAND SERVICE WEBSITES

HP MagCloud (www.magcloud.com)
In addition to showcasing and selling your publication on MagCloud's storefront through a browser-based viewer, from the HP MagCloud iPad app, or as a PDF download, readers can also opt to purchase a professional-quality, full-color glossy print version of your magazine

through the service. There is no cost to upload a publication, and after you've uploaded your PDF file (which has to be created to MagCloud specifications), you can then select your particular product (standard, flyer, pamphlet, digest, square, tabloid, or poster), trim size, and desired binding method (saddle stitched or perfect bound) for the print version of your magazine. Digital publications can either be distributed for free, free along with a print purchase, or offered for a fee. If you decide to set a fee, then proceeds will be split: 70 percent to you (the publisher) and 30 percent to MagCloud. Prices must at least be $1. Printed pages are charged at $0.20 per page with the ability for you to add in markup as you desire. MagCloud will take care of all the transactions, printing, shipping, and digital distribution for you. You can track sales and online readership, and a variety of social media sharing functions are available.

Issuu (www.issuu.com)
Issuu will convert your single-paged document (supported file types include PDF, DOC, PPT, ODT, WPD, SXW, RTF, ODP and SXI) into a beautiful online publication (The quality is amazing!) that will be displayed on their website. Uploading a document requires you to add publication information such as:

- Title
- Description
- Web name or URL
- Keywords
- Document type (article or essay, book, catalog, magazine, newspaper, report, etc.)
- Category (Auto & Vehicles, Business & Marketing, Creative, Film & Music, Fun & Entertainment, Hobby & Home, Knowledge & Resources, Nature & Animals, News & Politics, Nonprofits & Activism, Religion & Philosophy, Sports, Technology & Internet, Travel & Events, Weird & Bizarre, or Other)

- Allow comments (yes or no)
- Allow ratings (yes or no)
- Allow publication download (yes or no)

It is important that the information you provide is both accurate and correct so that your magazine can be properly indexed by search engines and appropriately displayed for visitors browsing through Issuu's website. Functions include download, print, zoom, search capability, RSS integration, and search engine optimization. In addition, readers can add comments, "Like" a publication, as well as share content via Facebook, Twitter, Google+, or email. An embed code is also provided in case you wish to embed the publication into your own website. Detailed statistics that give insight into reader behavior include how many views, bookmarks, ratings, comments, and links you receive as well as where in the world your readers are located. A mobile version is available for Android, with the promise of an iOS app soon to come. Issuu is best suited for publishers who wish to display sneak previews or free editions of their ad-supported magazines. Issuu comes in a free, ad-supported version. Priced at $19 a month, the Pro version includes unlimited bandwidth, 15GB storage, no sidebar display of related publications, and the omission of banner advertising.

Joomag (www.joomag.com)
With Joomag, you can either upload an original single-paged PDF document or use their versatile online editor that enables you to create your magazine from a template that can be modified by adding text, images, vector shapes, hyperlinks, video, audio, feedback forms, and galleries. I was quite impressed with how easy the tool was to use and the final result, which ended up looking rather slick and extremely professional. Magazines have the usual flip and zoom capabilities, file download and print ability, and HTML5 support. A native iPad application is available should readers prefer to view the magazine that way. It is also possible to embed the magazine into your website.

You can offer your publication for free or set a subscription price. Joomag will handle the administration function and charges a transaction fee of 30 percent of the selling price. Subscription management tools are available, and metrics are also provided. Plan prices start from free to $39.95 a month and above, depending on the features you select.

Yudu (www.yudu.com)
Yudu is a digital publishing library and marketplace that lets you read, publish, buy, sell, and share digital content such as magazines, brochures, catalogs, and other publications that have traditionally been published in print. Serving Web, mobile, and tablet platforms, Yudu provides tools that let you publish fully interactive digital content with the capability of adding video, audio, animation, slideshows, Twitter feeds, interactive competitions, and more. Various subscription management options are available, and you can deploy your magazine to app stores such as Apple's Newsstand, Google Play, and the Amazon Appstore. Publishers earn 75 percent of all sales. Features include print and zoom, panning, swiping, search, bookmarking, SEO optimization, reader behavior statistics, Google Analytics integration (for Web editions), and the ability to share your favorite pages directly from the toolbar to networks such as Facebook, Twitter, Google+, and LinkedIn. Yudu will even host your publication for free. The Pro version is priced at approximately $150 a year, and there is a scaled-down free version also available online.

Customized Apps for iOS and Android Devices

The following services allow you to create fully customized magazine apps without the need or expense of hiring an iOS or Android developer. These platforms provide simple, do-it-yourself solutions that allow you to take your PDF and create a totally branded, fully interactive experience that can be made available and ready for purchase from Apple's App Store, Google Play, or the Amazon Appstore. As you decide what platforms you will use to deliver your app, you might want to take into consideration that according to predictions from Forrester Forecast (www.forrester.com), 760 million people globally will own a tablet by 2016 (including one-third of Americans), and 53 percent of those tablets will be iPads. (See Figure 9.)

CUSTOMIZED APP SOLUTIONS

App Studio by Quark (www.appstudio.net)
App Studio is a cloud-based solution that lets you take documents created with familiar software, such as QuarkXPress and InDesign, and transform them into interactive (HTML5) content that is ready to be made into a fully branded app on the device of your choice. App Studio creates hybrid apps, which means that it takes the native code of each platform (e.g., iOS) and combines it with HTML5 to give users an experience that incorporates the best of both worlds. As you can expect from a software company that's been around for over thirty years, App Studio's features are quite extensive, offering interactivity such as slideshows, video, audio, animation, 360-degree photography, scroll zones, cross-linking, swiping, pinching, zooming, and more. The Multi-Issue Pro plan requires your publication to be designed in QuarkXPress and is priced at around $110 a month for one publication with unlimited issues. This program includes apps for the iPad, iPad mini, iPhone, and Kindle Fire. The Multi-Issue Premium plan, where your publication can be designed in either QuarkXPress or InDesign, is priced at around $550 a month for one publication with unlimited issues; this plan includes apps for the iPad, iPad mini, iPhone, Kindle Fire, Android tablet, and Android smartphone. A free 30-day trial is available online.

Figure 9: Global Tablet Installed Base by OS (millions)

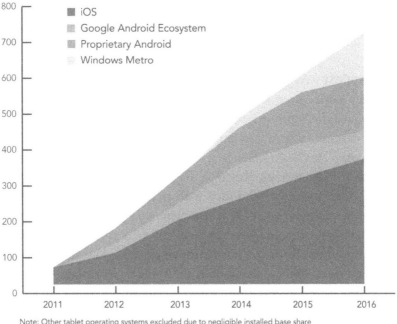

Note: Other tablet operating systems excluded due to negligible installed base share
(number of units actually in use).
Source: Forrester Forecast, April 2012

Mag+ (www.magplus.com)

Mag+ is primarily an InDesign plug-in (created as an alternative to Adobe's Digital Publishing Suite) that lets you create your own customized tablet and smartphone apps that include dynamic content, interactivity, video, sound, and HTML objects without the need for any programming skills whatsoever. The Mag+ Reviewer App is free for download from Apple's App Store, Google Play, and Amazon's Appstore. It lets you view and test your app to see what it looks like and how it performs on the platform of your choice between the iPad, iPhone, Android, or Kindle Fire. You then assemble, build, and configure your app using the web-based tool Mag+ Publish, and from there, you can publish to the app store of your choice. One app on one device with unlimited issues is priced at $399 a month. You can publish to an additional device for an extra $99 a month or publish to all devices for an extra $199 a month.

MagCast (www.magcasting.co)
MagCast is a complete publishing system that allows you to publish your magazine as your own branded and customized app directly to Apple's Newsstand, where you can sell individual issues or subscriptions as "In-App Purchases." First you will need to convert your magazine issue into a PDF format. Keynote, Pages, and PowerPoint templates are provided for those who may wish to jump-start the magazine design process. When your PDF is complete, you then upload it to MagCast, where you can add interactive content such as links, video, and audio components. After you have finished editing and testing and are ready to go live, you simply publish to Apple's Newsstand with the push of a button. MagCast provides an extensive training course on how to best use the system for seamless integration with Newsstand. It is necessary for you to sign up for an Apple Developer account (priced at $99 a year) to use the service, and there's a tutorial that will walk you through the entire application process. MagCast is priced at $297 a month, which allows for the publishing of one iPad magazine with no limit on the number of issues or edits you can make. As the publisher, you receive all revenue generated from your publication (except for Apple's customary 30 percent, which it takes on all apps listed in the App Store). MagCast apps are specifically formatted for, and only suitable to be viewed on, the iPad and iPad mini. The platform also allows for Google Analytics integration.

TapEdition (www.tapedition.com)
TapEdition allows you take a PDF file and use their platform to add interactive features such as video, audio, photo galleries, information pop-ups, maps, external web links, internal page links, and RSS feeds.

In addition, the service allows for In-App purchasing and renewable subscriptions, with all payments being processed through Apple. TapEdition is priced at $499 a month for an iPad and iPhone universal app, which includes unlimited issues and unlimited changes. If you also require an Android app that will work on both Android smartphones and tablets, then the service will cost an additional $199 a month.

Proofing Your Magazine

When you have the final version of your digital magazine in your hands, or should I say on your screen, then congratulations are due; but don't hit the publish button just yet. I suggest you thoroughly go through your magazine and proofread it both slowly and carefully. No matter how many times you have read, proofread, and edited the documents, after the magazine is laid out in its final form, it is likely that you will still find errors that were previously missed.

Have your colleagues read through and supply corrections too. It is a good idea to have a fresh pair of eyes look over your final layout, so you may wish to hire a professional proofreader to give it the once-over as well. Compile a list that contains all the page numbers and accurately describe any problems you find. When your list is compiled, make the changes yourself, or if you used a designer for the job, have him or her make the changes and then proof it again. Reiterate the process until you're satisfied that your magazine is error free and ready to publish. Here is a list of items to check before you publish:

- Check that page numbers appear in the correct sequence, in the correct location, and on the correct pages
- Check that the page numbers listed in the table of contents correspond to the correct pages throughout the magazine
- Examine headlines, subheads, photo captions, and display type for correct information, wording, typos, fonts, spacing, and placement

- Read stories out loud, checking for misspelled words, typing errors, missing or broken words and sentences, and incorrect punctuation
- Check that graphics are scaled and cropped correctly; that they appear in the right places, alongside the correct stories; and that they are not blurred or out of focus (unless that's the desired effect)
- Check audio and video files to ensure they are embedded correctly (no missing files or links) and appear alongside the correct stories
- Test the zoom function on text and images to ensure sharpness of items and legibility
- Test hyperlinks to ensure they are pointed to the right web addresses
- Click on hotspots and pop-ups to ensure they function properly and link to information as expected
- Check advertiser placements and correctness of files, links to sites, etc. (This is very important.)
- Check for extra spaces and blank lines throughout the text
- Check column spacing and alignment through the publication
- Check the gutter spacing (the white space formed by the inner margins of two facing pages) on all pages and spreads
- Check that the correct issue number, date, and price is displayed on the cover and on the inside of the magazine

Chapter 11:
Monetizing Your Magazine

Magazine-a-nomics

Unless this is a labor of love, I should imagine that eventually you'd like to see your magazine turn a profit, maybe even to the point where you can finally quit that day job. But hold your horses; there's a lot that has to happen before you can get to that point.

The first thing you'll need to do is figure out how much revenue your magazine needs to generate before you consider it as being profitable. The way to do that is by first estimating your costs. As the saying goes, "It takes money to make money," so you can expect to incur up-front expenses. You should plan for these in advance so that you can safely keep yourself afloat before you begin to realize a return.

In the beginning, your costs will be divided into four sections: start-up costs, production costs, fixed costs, and variable costs. Your start-up costs will include everything you initially need to get your magazine off the ground. Items like the business license and registration fees, trademark registration, and any equipment or software you need to purchase to get your publication up and running would be considered as start-up costs.

Production costs cover everything it takes to get your magazine produced. You will need to pay for content, artwork (photography and illustrations), layout and design, editing, proofing, models, location expenses, props, etc.

Fixed costs remain the same regardless of the level of sales or activity within the business. Examples include rent, post office box rental fees, bank fees, the Internet connection charge, web hosting fees, and staff salaries.

Variable costs change in proportion to the level of sales or activity within the business. Examples include marketing and promotion activities, the cost of acquiring a commissioned salesperson (if you decide to go that route), and the fees associated with hiring freelancers such as photographers, web designers, or programmers.

Figure 10 gives a list of costs you may need to incur to start your business. Depending on your frequency of publication, you may want to work out the costs for an entire year and then break it down from there so that you can figure out the cost associated with producing each issue. It's very rare that a magazine will come out of the gate generating a profit. It will take time before you get into the groove editorially, spread the word, build a paid-subscriber list, and manage to garner the attention and trust of advertisers; but that is, of course, what you will be working toward all along.

Fill in the amounts as best you can. Having read the previous chapters, you should have enough information to make reasonably accurate assumptions as to what you will need to get your project off the ground. When you arrive at a final amount, then add in at least 25 percent to allow for any unforeseen expenses or inflation price hikes. It's better to be safe than sorry. There are four main sources of income for a magazine:

1. Advertising revenue
2. New and renewal subscription revenue
3. Single-copy sales
4. Ancillary income

The secret to calculating a magazine's required profit level is to estimate the costs and then figure out exactly how many single copies and subscriptions you need to sell, how much you need to charge per ad, and how many ads you need to sell per issue to eventually become profitable.

> **Tip:** According to the most recent statistics on averages calculated by the Association of Magazine Media from ABC Publishers Statements, print magazine distribution revenue indicated 27 percent derived from single-copy sales and 73 percent from subscriptions.

Don't be afraid of the numbers however, or aim to just skip over this section. Number crunching is never fun, but it's better to have an idea now so that you can realistically plan your finances and estimate what you will need to keep your magazine going rather than experience setbacks or surprises that can put your magazine permanently out of business later on down the line.

Most magazines start out containing little or no advertising, so it's expected that you won't be able to recoup all expenses and generate a profit from (at least) your first couple issues, but as your magazine grows and advertising sales pick up, ideally you should be able to recoup expenses over time. Your main focus during this time should be to heavily market your publication, build relationships, create communities, and increase readership; those are the factors that will ultimately determine your success. Entice readers to become loyal subscribers by offering a free issue, a free trial, or even a free subscription. Do whatever you need to do to grow your readership level and lock your readers in for the long term.

About Advertising

According to the Association of Magazine Media, magazine advertising–over both television and Internet advertising–is the most powerful medium for increasing purchase intent. Readers enjoy browsing

Figure 10: Start-up Costs Worksheet

Expense Type	Description	Amount ($)
Business	Business license and registration	
	Incorporation fee	
	Trademark registration	
	Banking fees	
	Rent/PO Box rental	
	Phone/Fax line rental	
	Internet broadband connection fees	
	Business card print charge	
	Misc.: Utilities, etc.	
Office Supplies	Pens, paper, stapler, envelopes, mailing labels, folders, printer ink, etc.	
Equipment	Computer/Laptop	
	Tablet	
	Smartphone	
	E-reader	
	Digital camera	
	Audio equipment (microphone, digital recorder, etc.)	
	Video equipment (video camera, tripod, etc.)	
	Multifunction printer	
	External backup hard drive	
	Memory card reader	
	Misc.: discs, storage cards, cables, batteries, equipment bags, etc.	
Website	Domain name registration	
	Hosting fees	
	Web designer/ Programmer/ Developer	
	Maintenance fee	
Software	Microsoft Office	
	Web design software or template	
	Website additional costs (shopping cart software, etc.)	

	WordPress (or other) theme	
	WordPress additional costs (membership plug-in, etc.)	
	Digital magazine creation software or service	
	Page layout and design software	
	Image editing software	
	Audio editing software	
	Video editing software	
	Misc.: Other software	
Design	Logo design	
	Business card layout and design	
	Media kit layout and design	
	Website layout and design or WordPress theme customization	
	Magazine layout and design	
Editorial (per issue)	Content	
	Artwork: Stock photography	
	Artwork: Photographer(s)	
	Artwork: Illustrator(s)	
	Artwork: Animator(s)	
	Videographer(s)	
	Audio Engineer(s)	
	Misc.: Editing, proofing, models, hair, makeup, etc.	
Salary Expense	Staff salaries	
Advertising	Marketing and promotion costs	
Professional Services	Consulting fees (Business consultant, lawyer, accountant, etc.)	
Miscellaneous Expenses	Production costs (i.e., Apple developer program enrollment fee, etc.)	
	Membership/Association/Conference fees	
	Training	
	Other	
TOTAL COSTS		**$**

through ads and consider them an integral part of magazines. A reader's feelings of connection and trust for a particular publication often creates a halo effect, and this feeling of goodwill is extended to the advertisers presented. As a result, readers are more likely to take action regarding the product or service being offered.

Advertisers buy space in a magazine to target particular niche markets that may be interested in purchasing their products or services. Most magazines depend on the revenue derived from advertising to pay costs and generate profits.

To find advertisers for your publication, check the competition to see who currently and consistently advertises with them. Your media kit will present potential advertisers with all the information they need to make an informed decision. As you do not have a track record to justify your prices, it is unlikely that you will be able to sell advertising to major companies or advertisers in your first issue. Instead, approach small businesses or websites that target your particular niche.

Initially, it may be worth giving a few ads away for free to increase credibility in the eyes of both your audience and your potential advertisers. However, the effort and cost of producing an ad may cause some advertisers to shy away from a free offer, so consider providing layout and design services at cost or for free as an added incentive. If you support a particular cause and would like to use a ready-made ad in your magazine, you can download free public service ads from PSA Central at psacentral.adcouncil.org.

THE DIFFERENT TYPES OF ADVERTISING

As a digital publication, there are numerous options available that you can use to monetize your magazine. Here are some of the most popular choices. As you explore these options, remember not to compromise, cheapen, or clutter your website or blog with too many annoying, obtrusive, distracting ads that take away from your content, which should always remain your primary focus. Without great content, you won't have readers, and without readers, you won't attract advertisers; so it's great content first and everything else after that.

In-page ads: Ads of specified sizes and dimensions that appear inside a magazine for a set fee

Newsletter ads: Allow you to monetize your newsletter by offering space to advertisers that provides them with direct access to your highly targeted email subscriber list

Classified ads: Low-priced small ads or announcements that usually appear at the back of a magazine

Advertorials or sponsored content: Advertisements that appear in editorial form and give information about a product or service but are designed to look like objective journalistic articles. Most publishers feel that these types of ads should be clearly labeled "advertising feature" or "paid advertisement" so as not to confuse or "trick" a reader and compromise integrity.

Sponsorship: Allowing a company to pay to be the only advertiser that appears within an issue, or a set number of issues, in a magazine

Paid content: Where you sell access to certain parts of your website

Google AdSense ads: A free, simple program that allows a publisher to earn money by displaying targeted Google text, image, video, or rich media ads on a website. Revenue is generated on a per-click (where an advertiser pays every time an ad is clicked) or per-impression (where an advertiser pays every time an ad is displayed regardless of whether it is clicked) basis.

Web banner ads: Ad images embedded into a web page that allow a visitor to click through to the associated site for more information. The advertiser pays the content provider somewhere around five to ten (U.S.) cents for every click the banner receives regardless of whether a purchase is made or not. Although this type of advertising is on the decline and not really conducive to smartphone viewing, plenty of banner exchange programs are available across the Web.

Affiliate program ads: Where you partner with an online merchant to receive a referral fee or commission from the conversions that occur when a customer clicks on the affiliate's link or banner ad and performs a desired action such as making a purchase or signing up for a newsletter

SETTING AD RATES

With no industry standard set as of yet on how to measure or price a digital ad, the easiest thing to do is to find out what rates digital magazines comparable to yours are charging. Go online and download their media kits (which should be readily available online). Study their rate sheets. Aim to offer slightly lower, competitive rates in order to attract or steal away (yes, this can be a dirty business) some of your competitors' advertisers.

After you have set your basic rates, it will be necessary to adjust them for special instances such as early payment, frequency discounts, the particular dimension selected, small business or nonprofit charges, agency discounts, and a special position charge for ads placed in prime positions (e.g., the inside front cover or within the first few pages of the magazine).

Once an ad has been sold and laid out in the magazine, make sure to send the advertiser a proof—whether it's a screen shot or otherwise—for his or her approval. You should create an advertiser agreement to facilitate the process. Also, I recommend that you not include the ad within the final layout of your magazine's design unless payment has been received in full.

SELLING THE ADS

In the beginning, it is likely that you will be selling most of the ads yourself. This is not a bad thing, as who knows your magazine better than you? Before making cold calls or sending out emails, learn as much as you can about your prospective advertiser and what his or her needs are, so you can persuasively tout the benefits of advertising with you.

Aim to sell ads by annual contract and offer the appropriate frequency discount. This way, you are not scrambling or desperate to find advertisers for every issue. Although this does not mean you should ever stop your quest for advertisers in your magazine, at least these will be pages you do not have to worry about generating income for in upcoming issues.

Know your media kit inside out so that you are ready to answer any questions a prospective advertiser might have. Although it may be frightening at first, after a few calls you will become much more confident and relaxed. Start with the prospects you are least interested in acquiring and use these as warm-up calls. Sound enthusiastic and excited about your magazine and the potential partnership. Ask questions to get them talking. Listen carefully to their answers to find out more about their marketing needs and fit them with what your magazine has to offer.

Think ahead and find any synergies you can exploit that may exist between the articles or particular themes that appear on your editorial calendar and the individual advertiser's products or services. Get advertisers excited about the new possibilities for multimedia and interactivity that digital now offers (i.e., click here to "Like" us on Facebook) and the types of analytics that can be reported about reader behavior, URL clicks, and unique page views. Let them know they will be a vital part of this new frontier. An Adobe-sponsored study conducted by Alex Wang, PhD (from the University of Connecticut, Stamford) found that interactive advertisements in digital magazines have higher engagement than static (print) ads, making readers more likely to interact with an ad and resulting in a higher probability that a purchase will actually be made.

Will you include a special advertiser page that appears within your magazine or on your website that showcases an advertiser's logo and provides a direct link to their site? Think of ways you can really add value and incorporate these as part of your enticing offer. Aim to create a win-win situation for both you and your potential advertiser.

Make sure to establish deadlines and specify what the next steps are. If local, I advise you pay your potential advertiser a visit. (Nothing beats face-to-face communication.) Otherwise, you should email your media kit, prototype, or a sample issue to provide them with the additional information they may need. Keep detailed notes of your call, so you can remember everything that was discussed and the actions that will be necessary for follow-up.

If you just cannot fathom carrying out the sales calls yourself, then think of other people who could possibly help you out. Consider hiring a sales rep, freelancer, stay-at-home mom, retiree, friend, college student–the possibilities are endless. All you need is someone who is enthusiastic about your project and has a great telephone manner. Compensation offered for the sale of an ad can range anywhere between 15 to 20 percent.

Note: According to a study by GfK MRI (www.gfkmri.com), 70 percent of tablet owners say they want to be able to buy items by clicking on an ad in a digital magazine. The survey further revealed that 73 percent of readers read or tapped on advertisements appearing in an electronic magazine; 47 percent took action after reviewing an ad (among respondents who could recall at least one ad), with 62 percent of those visiting an advertiser's website or retail store and 54 percent actually making, or considering, a purchase. These are stats and figures that your advertisers would be very interested to know, so take the time to educate and inform them. Consider including this type of information in your media kit.

Chapter 12:

Keeping It Legal

The Basics

To steer away from possible lawsuits, it is important to exercise sound judgment with your editorial decisions. Publishers and editors alike should acquire a basic understanding of the law as it applies to magazine publishing, with particular attention being paid to the following areas:

1. **Libel**
   Libel can be defined as "a published false statement that is damaging either to a person's reputation, a business, or a product." The key word in that sentence is *false*. This can mean inaccurate, untrue, or uncorroborated—the list goes on. All articles, references, headlines, photos, and illustrations should be examined thoroughly to diminish the likelihood of any legal liability.

2. **Invasion of privacy**
   People have the right to be left alone, have control of information published about them, and not be represented in a false light. Never obtain information using unscrupulous or questionable methods,

and always require a signed agreement that gives consent and grants permission for you to publish a story, interview, graphic, or illustration.

3. Copyright infringement and plagiarism
Copyright infringement is the unauthorized use of a copyrighted work. There is a provision, however, called "fair use," which allows for the limited use of a copyrighted work without an author's permission. Unfortunately, there are no hard-and-fast rules for the definition of fair use, so I would advise you practice restraint in the use of others' materials. "Borrowing," or using a couple of words in the creation of a new work, is different from lifting or quoting several paragraphs of information. You can also run into the issue of plagiarism, which is using someone else's work or ideas without acknowledgment and then falsely claiming them to be your own.

Contracts and Agreements

You need to prepare contractual agreements for anyone who works on or submits material to your magazine, including advertisers, writers, photographers, models, designers, illustrators, or any other freelancer you may hire. An agreement is exactly that: it is a clear outline of the terms upon which two parties agree to work together. It protects you from any lawsuits that could arise for such claims as copyright infringement, libel, or invasion of privacy.

Your signed contractual agreements should be saved forever, even if you decide to cease publishing. Although various contract examples can be found online, it is important that you consult with a lawyer for guidance on preparing the legal documents that will be necessary for your magazine.

Writer Agreements
In brief, your writer agreement grants you the right to print and publish a story. It outlines how much you will pay as well as your

rights to revise and edit a story. It requires that the author warrant he or she is the sole, original creator of the work. More importantly, the author has to agree to hold you, the publisher, harmless against any claim, demand, suit, or proceeding that may be brought against you for any reason in regards to his or her work.

Illustrator Agreements

Your illustrator agreement, much like your writer agreement, grants you the right to print and publish an illustration. It outlines how much you will pay and requires that the illustrator warrants that to the best of his or her knowledge the concepts, ideas, copy sketches, artwork, electronic files, and other materials produced do not infringe on any copyright or personal or proprietorial rights of others. They have to agree to hold you, the publisher, harmless against any claim, demand, suit, or proceeding that may be brought against you for any reason in regards to their work and that the work is considered a work for hire, where all concepts, ideas, copy, sketches, artwork, electronic files, and other materials related to the particular project become the property of the publisher.

Photography Agreements

When you work with a professional photographer, the photographer owns the image. Even though the image would not have been created if it were not for your assignment and you may have paid for its production, he or she still owns all rights to the image. Photographers make their living by selling the use of their work, not just by creating it. A standard usage agreement gives you the exclusive rights to use the image for a specified, agreed upon period of time. When that period has expired, the image is released from the agreement, and the photographer may sell usage of the image as stock or sell it outright to a buyer, or you can renegotiate for more time. Any commercial photographer can supply you with a usage agreement; it is not a form you have to create yourself.

Model Release Form

You should get a signed model release anytime your photo contains recognizable images of people. Publishing an identifiable photo of a person without a model release signed by that person can result in a civil liability for whoever publishes the photograph. A model release says the person being photographed has given consent to be photographed and grants his or her permission for the images to be used for the purposes outlined in the agreement.

Minor Release Form

Similar to a model release, a minor release form applies to a model under the age of 18, who is considered a minor, and requires the signature of a parent or legal guardian to give permission for the image to be used. It is a good idea to get both parents to sign if possible, as this reduces the risk that one parent will try to revoke the consent given by the other.

Trademarking Your Magazine's Name and Logo

A trademark is a distinctive word, name, mark, emblem, or symbol that is legally registered to identify the goods made or sold by a person or entity and to distinguish them from the goods made or sold by another person or entity. Although it is not absolutely necessary to register your name and logo, it is wise to do so. That way you can lock down and protect your magazine's title, notify others of its use and existence, and prevent other entities from using any similar names or symbols in the marketplace.

Trademark filing fees start from $275 depending upon the type of application submitted, and you can file online at the United States Patent and Trademark Office (www.uspto.gov). Although the process is not that difficult, I recommend you consult with a professional for advice beforehand. If you decide to file online, you will receive an electronic receipt within twenty-four hours via email that contains the serial number associated with your application. The entire process can take anywhere from thirteen to eighteen months to complete. While awaiting a definitive response, you can use the serial number provided to check the status of your application online.

Appendix A:
Essential WordPress Plug-ins

Note: The following plug-ins are available for free except where indicated.

Security

Because of WordPress's popularity and widespread use, the software is prone to hacker attacks, which can do anything from taking your blog completely offline for good to redirecting your traffic to another website altogether. Use the following plug-ins to help bulletproof your WordPress installation; always remember to use strong passwords for your admin panel that contain mixed-case letters, numbers, and symbols and are at least 10 characters in length.

Akismet
This tool helps combat comment spam. It comes standard with all WordPress installations but has to be set up and activated.

Antivirus

This antivirus protection software for your blog protects against malicious spam and code injections.

BackWPup

BackWPup schedules a complete WordPress backup to locations such as an FTP Server, Dropbox, SugarSync, Google Storage, or email.

Block Bad Queries (BBQ)

BBQ secures WordPress against hacker attacks.

Growmap Anti-Spambot Plug-in (GASP)

This plug-in all but eliminates comment spam by placing a checkbox on the comment submission form that spambots are unable to check off. This plug-in should stop 99 percent of all automated spam bots.

Search Engine Optimization (SEO)

Help your blog rank higher in search results by using any of the following plug-ins. Most users either install the All in One SEO Pack along with Google XML Sitemaps or just use WordPress SEO by itself, which includes sitemap generation. Sitemaps provide crawlers with a hierarchical list of pages that appear on a website so they can be found more easily.

All in One SEO Pack

With over 13 million downloads to date, All in One SEO Pack automatically optimizes your blog for search engines with several easy-to-use functions.

Google XML Sitemaps

This plug-in generates an XML sitemap that enables search engines like Google, Bing, Yahoo!, and Ask.com to better index your site.

WordPress SEO by Yoast

Considered the most complete WordPress SEO plug-in today, its features include optimization of page content, image titles, and meta descriptions as well as XML sitemap generation.

Membership

The following plug-ins promise to have your membership site up and running in no time.

Digital Access Pass (DAP)

You can create free or paid membership levels and provide different levels of access to content like WordPress pages, posts, and categories, video and audio files, PDF reports, MS Office docs, ZIP files, and HTML pages among others. You have the ability to sell recurring subscriptions or set up for a one-time sale product. DAP includes a free shopping cart for Authorize.net, Paypal Standard, and Paypal Website Payments Pro, so members can check out and pay directly from your website. DAP is priced at $167 for use on a single domain and $297 for use on an unlimited number of domains.

Magic Members

Magic Members includes unlimited membership levels and the ability to offer different membership access to different areas. Also, the download manager protects downloads from being accessed by unauthorized members. It features seamless integration with AWeber, GetResponse, Constant Contact, iContact, and MailChimp and integrates with numerous payment gateways: 1ShoppingCart, PayPal Standard, PayPal Website Payments Pro, PayPal Express Checkout, CCBill, Authorize.net, ClickBank, and WorldPay. Magic Members is priced at $97 for use on a single domain, $197 for use on up to three domains, and $297 for use on an unlimited number of domains.

WishList Member

WishList lets you create free, trial, or paid membership levels; develop "modular" memberships with the ability to hide content from other levels; and automatically expire a membership after a certain time period. It integrates with PayPal, ClickBank, and other online payment solutions. WishList is priced at $97 for use on a single domain and $297 for use on an unlimited number of (personal) domains.

Social Media Sharing

Use any of the following plug-ins to make it quick and easy for readers to share content with their social networks.

Digg Digg

This floating share bar has a ton of customizable options and lets your audience share with popular networks such as Facebook (also includes the Facebook "Like" button), Twitter, Buffer, Pinterest, Digg, LinkedIn, Google +1, reddit, TweetMeme, Topsy, Yahoo! Buzz, StumbleUpon, and Delicious.

ShareThis

ShareThis is a fully customizable share bar that allows for access to up to 120 social media channels. It includes email sharing capability and provides real-time analytics in the form of detailed reports, letting you track your most popular content and providing insight into social sharing behavior.

Slick Social Share Buttons

This plug-in lets you add Facebook, Twitter, Google +1, LinkedIn, Digg, Buffer, Delicious, reddit, and Pinterest social media buttons to your website in either a floating bar or a sliding panel; it also provides social metrics that can be viewed from the admin's social statistics page.

Related Posts

These plug-ins help to make your blog site "sticky" by listing related content that visitors can read or view.

nrelate Related Content

This plug-in uses patent-pending technology to continuously analyze a blog site's content and display other related content that appears on the site. You can easily customize the look of this plug-in by using one of the included set styles, or you have the option to design your own.

Yet Another Related Posts Plug-in (YARPP)

YARPP gives a list of posts or pages related to the current entry thereby introducing the reader to other relevant content on your site. It includes thumbnail support.

Miscellaneous

Broken Link Checker

The plug-in checks your posts, comments, and other content for broken links and missing images, and it sends out a notification either via the dashboard or by email.

Disqus Comment System

Disqus replaces your WordPress comment system with a tool that makes commenting and participating in discussions much easier and more interactive for your readers. It allows visitors to use their Facebook or Twitter accounts to leave comments on your blog.

Editorial Calendar by Zack Grossbart

This plug-in allows you to visually plan, schedule, and organize the upcoming posts for multiple authors through a graphical calendar-style user interface.

FD FeedBurner

This Google plug-in connects your WordPress RSS feed to Google's FeedBurner service. FeedBurner allows you to keep statistics on the people subscribing to your RSS feed, and it allows subscribers to receive postings by email. If set, it has the ability to automatically tweet your blog posts. Before you install this plug-in, it will be necessary to register your existing blog feed with FeedBurner (feedburner.google. com), at which point you will be given a replacement feed. A Google account is required for setup.

Google Analytics for WordPress

It adds Google Analytics to your blog site with numerous options.

Jetpack by WordPress.com

This heavy-weight WordPress plug-in provides a multitude of functions, including email subscriptions to blog posts and comments; automatic posting to social networks such as Twitter, Facebook, Tumblr, and LinkedIn; a recent tweets widget; and an artificial intelligence-based spelling, style, and grammar check tool.

NextGEN Gallery

NextGEN Gallery does just about everything you'd ever want to do with images over and above the basics that are offered by WordPress.

OIOPublisher

This powerful ad management software helps you maximize revenue, save time, and keep you in complete control of the ad space on your site. It integrates with payment options such as PayPal and 2Checkout. OIOPublisher is priced at $47.

TinyMCE Advanced

This is an advanced visual editor for WordPress that adds many features to the standard default editor, including the ability to compose a blog post in MS Word and then copy and paste it directly into WordPress. Not using this plug-in can cause problems, as Word adds in hidden code that can mess up the format of a post.

WPTouch

WPTouch automatically transforms your WordPress website into a mobile-friendly one for tablets and smartphones. There's also a Pro version available that comes with over two hundred more features than the free version and is priced at $49 for a one-domain license.

Appendix B:
Industry News and Resources

Ad Age (www.adage.com)
The leading global source of news, intelligence, and conversation for marketing and media communities

Affinity, LLC (www.affinityresearch.net)
Innovative marketing and media research company specializing in print and digital magazine accountability tracking

Alliance for Audited Media (www.auditedmedia.com)
Formerly known as the Audit Bureau of Circulations, the AAM is about industry professionals bringing accountability and confidence to the new world of media.

American Society of Magazine Editors (www.magazine.org/asme)
Founded in 1963, ASME works to defend the First Amendment, protect editorial independence, and support the development of journalism.

In addition, ASME sponsors the National Magazine Awards, the annual Best Cover Contest, and the Magazine Internship Program.

The Association of Magazine Media (www.magazine.org)
Formerly known as the Magazine Publishers of America (MPA), the association is a nonprofit resource that provides facts, data, and research on the magazine industry.

Coverjunkie (www.coverjunkie.com)
Coverjunkie is all about creativity and inspiration. The website highlights the most creative magazine cover designs from around the world.

eMedia Vitals (www.emediavitals.com)
Online magazine for web and digital media experts

FIPP (www.fipp.com)
Worldwide magazine media association

Folio Magazine (www.foliomag.com)
Magazine publishing industry news and information resource

GfK Mediamark Research & Intelligence (www.gfkmri.com)
Producer of media and consumer research in the United States

LinkedIn Magazine Publishing Group (linkd.in/Y259FB)
Created for publishing professionals from all over the world, this LinkedIn group currently consists of over 32,000 members. You need to be a member of LinkedIn to join.

McPheters & Company (www.mcpheters.com)
McPheters & Company specializes in strategic planning and research for brands and companies in media-related fields, including media owners, advertisers, and ad agencies.

MinOnline (www.minonline.com)
Covering media, publishing, and magazine news, min is the industry's trusted source on the consumer and B2B magazine business.

Mr. Magazine (www.mrmagazine.com)
Website and blog of magazine industry expert Samir Husni

Online Publishers Association (OPA) (www.online-publishers.org)
A not-for-profit trade organization dedicated to representing high-quality online content providers before the advertising community, the press, the government, and the public

The Pew Internet & American Life Project (www.pewinternet.org)
A nonpartisan, nonprofit "fact tank" that provides information on the issues, attitudes, and trends shaping America and the world

Publishing Executive (www.pubexec.com)
Provides vital information to publishing and production professionals on matters relating to printing, production, eMedia, and more.

The State of the News Media (www.stateofthemedia.org)
The Pew Research Center's Project for Excellence in Journalism offers this annual report about the major trends and key findings on American journalism.

Glossary

Ad sales rep: Person responsible for making sales calls and setting up appointments with existing and prospective advertisers. Also in charge of maintaining current accounts and generating new business.

Advertising director: Manages a staff of ad sales reps. Responsible for generating advertising in the magazine through direct selling and promotional activities.

Alt attribute: The text description of an image that is displayed when a mouse hovers over the image on the web.

Anchor text: The visible text (that usually appears underlined and in blue) on a web page that connects to either another web page, a graphic, a download, or another section of the page. When hovering over a clickable link, the cursor changes into a hand pointer.

Android: A Linux-based operating system developed by Google and designed for touchscreen mobile devices such as smartphones and tablets.

Ancillary income: A product or service a publisher can sell in addition to the magazine to raise awareness and generate additional income.

Animation: A simulation of movement created by displaying a series of independent pictures or frames.

App: Short for application. The term typically describes a software program that is used by a smartphone or mobile device.

Art director: Oversees the artistic design of the magazine and works closely with the editorial director to ensure the design is consistent with the editorial philosophy.

Associate editor: A staff editorial person who supports and assists the editor; writing, editing, and assigning material as required. May also be responsible for composing titles, subtitles, and captions.

Atom feed: Allows you to syndicate or distribute headlines from a blog, podcast, or website to a web feed.

Attribute: Refers to the properties that supply additional information about an HTML element. For instance, the <img> tag is used to display an image on a web page and can have various attributes, such as height, width, border size, border color, etc. For a real-world example, if a tag were a dress suit, then the attributes could be blue color, wool fabric, medium size, and gold buttons.

Audit bureau: An organization that audits and verifies a publisher's claimed circulation numbers.

Authority site: A popular site that is frequently visited, contains large amounts of strong content, has numerous incoming links based on merit and relevance, and is often referred to as a trusted source. Amazon.com, Wikipedia.com, and YouTube.com are all examples of authority sites.

Autoresponder: Computer software or configuration that automatically responds to an incoming email.

Backlinks: Incoming links to a website or web page.

Black hat SEO: Unethical and unacceptable search engine optimization practices that are not approved of by search engine companies.

Blacklist: A database of Internet addresses, or IPs, known to be used by spammers and denied a particular privilege, service, access, or recognition.

Bleed: Artwork or color that extends off the edge of the page of a magazine's layout.

Blog: An interactive website on which an individual or a group of users publish thoughts; share views, ideas, and opinions; discuss issues; divulge information; give advice; report on breaking news; provide useful links, photos, and videos; or share expertise and knowledge.

Blogger: A person who writes, publishes, and updates a blog.

Blogging: The act of writing, publishing, and updating a blog.

Blogroll: A list of blogs recommended by a blogger, which can appear as a sidebar menu on a blog site.

Body copy: The main text of a story.

Body type: The font used for body copy.

Browser incompatibility: When a website displays incorrectly depending on the browser, browser version, platform, or device it is being viewed on.

Business manager: Supervises internal office management.

Circulation: The number of readers a publication has.

Clickable link: A graphic or a portion of text (that usually appears underlined and in blue) on a web page that connects to either another web page, a graphic, a download, or another section of the same document in which the link appears. When hovering over a clickable link, the cursor changes into a hand pointer.

CMYK: The four ink colors used for printing, namely cyan (blue), magenta (red), yellow, and black. The four inks are combined in different quantities to reproduce and print (almost) all colors. The term CMYK is also described as either four color or process color.

Column: Articles that are usually written by an expert or a famous or respected individual. They provide credibility for the magazine and are written by the same person every issue.

Compatibility testing: Testing to ensure that a web page (or computer application) appears and behaves the same regardless of the operating system, browser, or device being viewed on.

Consumer magazine: Consumer magazines are general or special interest magazines that are marketed to the public. They are usually available via newsstand or subscription and more often than not contain advertising. The main purpose of these types of magazines is to entertain, sell products, and promote viewpoints. Examples include *Reader's Digest*, *i-D*, and *O, The Oprah Magazine*.

Content management system (CMS): Computer software or system used for organizing, managing, storing, and facilitating the creation of documents and other digital assets. Content management systems can either be online or offline.

Contributing editors: Writers who are experts in the field the magazine covers. Regular freelance writers with whom the magazine wishes to maintain a relationship with may also be given this title.

Conversion: A conversion is defined as the number of visitors who complete a desired action beyond just surfing and perusing a website.

Conversion rate: The rate at which a casual visitor to a website is either converted into a customer or takes some type of desired action such as make a purchase, sign up for a newsletter, subscribe to an RSS feed, or download a file.

Copy editor: Copy editors are not proofreaders. They check written material in its original form (before layout and design), looking for and correcting errors in grammar, spelling, usage, and style. They also check articles for form, length, and completeness.

Copyright infringement: The use of a copyrighted work, in whole or in part, without the original copyright holder's permission.

Copyright: Protects original works of authorship from use without permission.

CPM (cost per thousand readers): Used by print magazines to indicate the cost for an advertiser to reach 1,000 readers, calculated by dividing the page price by circulation. For example, if you have 5,000 readers and charge $1,000 per page, then CPM = $1,000 / 5 = $200.

Crawler: An automated software program that scans the Web with the purpose of storing and indexing web page information for search results.

CSS (cascading style sheets): A style language that defines the format and layout of an HTML document.

Defamation of character: Can include libel, slander, or both.

Department: The parts or sections of a magazine that a reader becomes familiar with and expects to see in every issue. They offer consistency and establish the tone and voice of a publication. A department may be written by a different contributor every month. They are grouped together under one common topic, so that an individual department may have one or several articles.

Design: The art of visual communication; utilizing color, type, illustration, photography, and layout techniques to present content or information that communicates effectively and is aesthetically pleasing to the eye.

Digital magazine: A highly interactive digital interpretation of a print magazine that can be read on an electronic device.

Editorial assistant: An entry-level employee who supports the more senior editors by performing duties such as researching information, setting up interviews, returning calls, making copies, and filing.

Editorial calendar: A schedule of the editorial content that is to be featured in upcoming issues. This information is used by advertisers to determine what issues or themes may best offer product or service tie-ins.

Editorial director: Person responsible for all final editorial decisions and for managing and coordinating the creative staff to ensure that the publication's editorial philosophy is executed and fulfilled with each issue.

Editorial philosophy: A mission statement that describes a magazine's main focus and reason for being.

Executive editor: Reports directly to the editorial director. Performs both managerial and editorial duties, keeping the magazine on schedule by enforcing strict deadlines.

Exit page: The last page visited by a reader before leaving a website.

Fact-checker: Researches submitted articles and checks to make sure information presented is accurate and correct.

Fair use: Allows for the limited use of copyrighted material without the need for an author's permission.

Feature: These are the longer pieces that appear in a magazine. In a print magazine these pieces are usually four to six pages in length. They are unique to every issue and most clearly exhibit the magazine's concept.

Flash: A vector animation software developed by Adobe and used by web designers to create animated websites containing graphics, games, cartoons, and movies.

Font: A particular typeface, including upper and lowercase letters, numbers, punctuation, and special characters.

Freelancer: Person who sells or contracts their work to various clients rather than being employed by one particular company.

Frequency: The number of times a year a magazine is published.

Frequency discount: A reduced advertising rate based upon the number of times an ad is placed in a magazine within a specified time period.

Google Analytics: A free web analytics solution created by Google that gives insight into website traffic, performance, and marketing effectiveness.

Google PageRank: A method used by Google to calculate the relevance and importance of a web page by measuring the quantity and quality of incoming links.

Graphic designer: A visual communicator who combines color, type, illustration, photography, animation, and video using various layout techniques to create a design that effectively communicates and appeals to its intended audience.

Hashtag: Used as a special symbol on various social media sites to mark a specific keyword or topic in a way that makes it easy for people to find or follow a "conversation" on that topic.

Header tags: HTML tags that help draw attention to important information on a web page such as the headline. Keywords contained within header tags can provide a rankings boost in search engine results.

Hot spot: A touch point or icon on a screen that is sensitive to selection and provides a link to additional information such as text or video.

HTML (hypertext markup language): A computer programming language designed and used to create web pages.

HTML5: The latest version of HTML that moves away from previous limitations and allows for much more dynamic functionality such as embedding audio and video, and displaying animations without the need for external plug-ins such as Adobe Flash.

Hyperlink: See *Clickable link.*

Inbound links: Incoming links to a website or web page.

Indexing: A data structure that allows information to be conveniently indexed to a database schema for efficient retrieval.

iOS: The operating system used by Apple on mobile devices such as the iPhone, iPod Touch, and iPad.

JavaScript: A simple programming language often used in conjunction with HTML, or other web programming languages, in order to make web pages more interactive.

Keyword prominence: The location or placement of a keyword in the source code of a web document. The higher up on the page or tag a keyword is, the more weight it is given by a search engine.

Keyword proximity: The closeness between two or more keywords.

Keyword research tool: A tool that helps select the most appropriate and effective keywords for a website.

Keyword rich: When a web page is full of relevant keywords.

Keyword stuffing or spamming: The process of adding a superfluous amount of keywords to a web page in such a way that the information ends up being nonsensical and user-unfriendly.

Keyword term or phrase: The specific term or phrase entered into a search engine by a user to search for information online.

Landing pages: A report that shows the most popular pages upon which visitors entered a site.

Layout: The way in which text or pictures are arranged on a page.

Leading: The space between the lines of type or copy on a page.

Libel: A published false statement that is damaging to either a person's reputation, a business, or a product.

Link text: See *Anchor text.*

Link: See *Clickable link.*

Logo: A distinguishing mark, emblem, or symbol that is used to identify an organization.

Long tail keywords: Keyword phrases of three words or more that allow for a narrow and distinct search for information online.

Marketing director: Also known as the promotions director. This individual is responsible for the publicity and promotion of a magazine.

Media kit: Magazine promotional tool, consisting of information on a magazine such as the audience demographics, market analysis, editorial calendar, and the advertising rate sheet.

Meta tags: Special HTML or XML tags (or coding statements) used by search engines to provide information about the contents of a web page.

Microblog: A simple Internet technology that allows a user to post short statements or sentences. Twitter (www.twitter.com) is an example of a microblogging service.

Mission statement: Statement that explains a company's aims, values, and reason for being.

Multimedia: Multiple forms of media, such as text, graphics, and sound, that are integrated together in some form.

News aggregator: A website or computer software that aggregates a specific type of information or news from multiple online sources.

Newsgroup: A place where people meet online to post ideas, ask questions, and comment on a particular topic.

Newsletter: A periodic publication distributed digitally via email to an opt-in list of subscribers.

Niche market: A narrowly defined group of potential customers for a magazine's particular subject matter.

Online community: A virtual community that consists of people who share common interests and use the Internet (websites, forums, chat rooms, email, etc.) to communicate, exchange, or collaborate online.

Other magazines: Magazines that cannot be defined as being either consumer or trade fall into this category.

Outbound links: Links within a website that point to an external source.

Page views: A statistic that shows the most popular pages that have been viewed on a website.

Perfect-bound: Adhesive binding where printed pages are shaved along the side and glued together at the spine.

Permalink: A URL that points to a specific blog post after it has passed from the front page into the archives.

Photo editor: Person responsible for assigning visuals and images to magazine stories. Can also be tasked with maintaining, cataloging, and storing images.

Ping: The act of notifying search engines, directories, and other services of new and fresh content that appears on a website or blog.

Plug-in: A software component that provides additional functionality or capabilities to a larger software application.

Podcast: A pre-recorded audio or video file that can either be streamed or made available for download online, and listened to or viewed on a personal computer or mobile device.

Podcatcher: An application that automatically checks for and downloads new podcasts via an RSS or XML feed.

Point size: The unit of measurement used to describe the size of type and leading. There are seventy-two points to an inch.

Pop-up: Allows for a digital publisher to hide text or imagery on a page.

Production director: Responsible for creating, coordinating, and overseeing the production schedule to ensure that the magazine is produced on time. Helps staff members format material so all pages are complete and technically accurate. May also oversee the magazine's press run.

Promotions director: See *Marketing director*.

Proofreader: Checks over the final proof for typographical errors.

Psychographic information: The study and classification of people according to their attitudes, aspirations, values, beliefs, and other psychological criteria.

Publication: A book, magazine, newspaper, journal, or musical piece.

Publisher: Oversees the business side of the magazine and is ultimately responsible for the magazine's profitability. Duties include budgeting, strategic planning, and ad development.

Rate sheet: Summarizes a publisher's prices for ads of different sizes and placement positions within the magazine. The rate sheet also provides frequency discount information.

Resolution: The sharpness of an image.

RGB: The primary additive colors of red, green, and blue. When these colors are combined equally they produce white, and when they are combined in different amounts they can produce a broad array of colors. TV and computer monitors produce images using the RGB method.

Rights-managed stock photography: A photo that is licensed for one-time, specific use only.

Robot: Software that scans the Web with the purpose of indexing pages for search results.

Robots.txt: A simple text file that tells a search engine not to crawl or index specified files or directories on a website.

Royalty-free stock photography: Allows for the unlimited use of a photo (or illustration) in any medium as defined by the licensing agreement.

RSS (Really Simple Syndication or Rich Site Summary): Allows for the syndication or distribution of content, or a summary of content, to subscribers who are automatically notified every time new content is added to either a blog, website, or podcast series. The information is displayed through an RSS reader or news aggregator.

RSS feed: An XML document that displays content, or a summary of content, published from a website and presents this information in a standardized format.

RSS subscription: The process of subscribing to and receiving a particular RSS feed.

Saddle stitch: Process where magazine pages are secured through the centerfold by wire staples.

Sans serif: Fonts that are straight and have no serifs, or curlicues, at the end of letters; generally used for headlines, subheads, and sidebars.

Search engine: A tool on the Internet that is used to search for and display relevant information.

Search engine-friendly: Coding a web page in a way that makes it easily accessible and understandable to search engine spiders.

Search engine optimization (SEO): The process of improving the visibility of a website or web page in a search engines' natural or unpaid organic search results.

Search engine rankings: The position of a web page returned in search results when searched for with a specific keyword or keyword phrase.

Senior editor: Writes, edits, proofreads, and copyedits articles. Helps assign articles to writers, making sure they understand the specifics. Other names for this title can include feature editor, beauty editor, fashion editor, and so forth.

Serif: Fonts that have curlicues at the end of the letters, which make them easier to read. Serif fonts are generally used for body text.

Short tail keywords: A one- or two-word search term, like the term "digital camera," that has a high search volume and is not very specific.

Slander: A false spoken statement that is damaging to either a person's reputation, a business, or a product.

Social bookmark: A way for users to share bookmarks through a social network such as StumbleUpon (www.stumbleupon.com).

Social media: An interactive website that functions as a virtual community and allows a user to set up a profile and create, share, and exchange information or ideas with others online.

Social media marketing: The process of gaining traffic or attention through the use of social media.

Spider: An automated software program that scans the Web with the purpose of storing and indexing web pages for search results.

Staff writer: Resident staff member who writes and contributes articles to the magazine.

Stock photography: Ready-made images that usually have to be purchased and are made available for immediate download online.

Tag: An HTML coding statement.

Target market: A specific group of customers or a particular market segment that a product or service is marketed to.

Text link: Text on a web page that is usually underlined or highlighted, appears in blue, and is used as a clickable link, or hyperlink.

Trackback: An automated alert that is sent to a blog owner to let him or her know that a post has been linked to or referenced from another site.

Trade magazines: Trade magazines are business-to-business magazines. The audience consists of readers in a particular trade or profession.

Trademark: A trademark is a distinctive word, name, mark, emblem, or symbol that is legally registered to identify the goods made or sold by a person or entity and differentiates them from the goods made or sold by another person. Trademarks grant exclusive rights to the owner that prevent competitors from using similar marks in the marketplace.

Traffic source: A report that provides an overview of the different kinds of sources (or websites) that send traffic to a site.

Typeface: See *Font*.

Typography: The art or process of setting and arranging type.

Unique visitors: Statistic that shows how many different people visit a website within a fixed time frame.

URL (Uniform Resource Locator): The address of a web page on the Web.

Visit duration: Web statistic that shows how long visitors spend on a site (in increments of seconds) and how many pages were viewed within that time.

Visitor path: See *Click path*.

Web designer: Responsible for the creation, design, layout, and coding of a web page.

Web host: A service or company that allows individuals and organizations to display websites that can be accessed over the Internet. Web hosts store HTML pages (and other types of code) on their servers.

Web maintenance agreement: An agreement to allocate a specified number of hours that a website will be worked on in a specified period of time (week or month, etc.) for a certain fee.

Website: A collection of web pages or other digital assets that is relative to a common URL.

Website editor: Responsible for creating and editing web content.

Web statistics: Software program that gathers and analyzes information on the behavior of website visitors, providing graphical statistical data on information such as what sites visitors came from, what day and time they visited, how long they stayed on each page, and what path they took through a site, etc.

Website compatibility: Ensuring that a website displays and acts the same regardless of what browser, browser version, platform, or device it is being viewed on.

WordPress: A web-based, open-source content management system (CMS) or blogging platform.

Writer's guidelines: Document created by a magazine for potential or interested contributors that describes exactly what the publisher is looking for in articles in order for them to be considered for publication.

XML Sitemap: Sitemaps provide crawlers with a hierarchical list of pages that appear on a website so they can be found more easily.

About the Author

Lorraine Phillips attended Jackson State University, where she acquired an MBA in business administration and a BS in computer science, graduating both programs with honors and distinction. She later went on to acquire an AA in graphic design from Bauder College and was elected to *Who's Who Among Students in American Colleges* for outstanding merit and accomplishments.

Lorraine is a creative information technology professional with over twelve years' experience in planning, developing, and publishing print, Internet, and digital projects. After serving as editorial director of *SisterPower Online* for nine years, she then launched *SisterPower Magazine* and was able to go directly from idea to newsstand after landing three distribution deals on the very first attempt.

Lorraine is currently CEO and founder of 360 Books, where she coaches and advises publishers, entrepreneurs, and business leaders on the best practices for online marketing and promotion through the smart, strategic use of today's technologies. She specializes in social media marketing, web content strategy development, branding, and design. Lorraine is available for consultations, speaking engagements, lectures, and seminars anywhere you might be across the globe. For more information, visit www.lorraine-phillips.com.

Index

N

O

P

Q

R

S